Bridget Clare McKeever, SSL, PhD

Hidden Addictions
A Pastoral Response
to the Abuse of Legal Drugs

Pre-publication
REVIEWS,
COMMENTARIES,
EVALUATIONS . . .

"**D**r. McKeever pulls no punches as she identifies some of the key cultural norms in our society that contribute to the hidden addictions of 'legal drugs' in American society.

After a short, crisp analysis of the problem and discussion of the dynamics of dependency, *Hidden Addictions* reveals the critical role that a male-oriented society plays in the lives of women in particular. But Dr. McKeever goes further to courageously identify the spiritual roots of this problem including some key problems within the church itself.

Despite the unique addictions found in the church, Dr. McKeever also finds within religious systems abundant resources that can be utilized to address these systemic problems.

The creative and insightful suggestions for a pastoral response make this a valuable aid for both clergy and lay counselors alike."

Rev. Dr. David W. Randle
President and CEO,
UCC Wellness Health
and Lifestyle Education Center,
Sandy, UT

"**T**here is an adage that a quick peek into a person's medicine cabinet provides an uncomfortably accurate assessment of their psychological health as well as of their medical status. *Hidden Addictions* provides a glimpse into the worlds of abuse and addiction that a peep into a medicine cabinet might suggest. However, the glimpse that this text provides is many steps removed from the world of guess, conjecture, and pop psychology. Bridget McKeever writes with the mind of an educator and the heart of a clinician. The value of this text is her ability to look at the problem of substance abuse from the differing perspectives of sociology, psychology, and spirituality as she develops a pastoral response to this individual as well as societal problem. *Hidden Addictions* is a must-read for physicians, pastors, nurses, and counselors. It should be required reading in every seminary and Clinical Pastoral Education program."

Martin C. Helldorfer, DMin
Vice President, Mission,
Leadership Development
and Corporate Culture,
Catholic Health Initiatives—
Eastern Region,
Aston, PA

"**D**r. McKeever has written a very helpful and needed resource for pastors and pastoral care specialists who are often involved with persons and their families concerning the abuse of legally prescribed and over-the-counter drugs. She helpfully analyzes the complexity and scope of the problem and demonstrates the ways it affects persons of all ages. Her documentation is chilling as she describes the risks and incidence of abuse, particularly among youth and young adult girls and boys, middle-age women, and elders. The vignettes describing the systemic dimensions of addiction in families and the complexity of pastoral responses demonstrate Dr. McKeever's pastoral skill and help readers connect with the reality of the problem. The social and spiritual analyses make the book a helpful resource for seminary classrooms as well as pastor's studies and church libraries."

Nancy J. Ramsay, PhD
Harrison Ray Anderson
Professor of Pastoral Theology,
Louisville Seminary,
Louisville, KY

More pre-publication
REVIEWS, COMMENTARIES, EVALUATIONS . . .

"**T**his short book could act as a good checklist for pastoral ministers and church staff to evaluate our own cultural and gender prejudices in dealing with sufferers who come to us. Many of us will not be alert to the signs and patterns of over-the-counter or prescribed drugs' destructive effects—something spelled out usefully here both in descriptive terms and in conversation scenarios.

Most of us will be quick to seize on McKeever's assertion that, 'Not only individual caregivers but also churches and synagogues are wounded healers.' What will undoubtedly be more difficult but ultimately more useful will be to accept her repeated urging that unless both ministers and medical personnel back off from masculinizing and medicalizing women's life problems, we will not only be 'wounded healers' but also 'wounded wounders.'

Bridget Clare McKeever has offered those of us who are ready to wrestle with this underlying problem as well as the chemical addiction problems enough stimulation and facts to start us on a better course for truly liberating and constructive ministry. This book takes the notorious adage, 'Better living through chemistry' and turns it around to urge, 'Better pastoring through understanding why people turn to chemistry.' Pick up the book and gauge your usual response to clients with problems against what it reveals."

Rev. Patrick Thompson, STD
Pastor,
St. Margaret Mary Catholic Church,
Lomita, CA

The Haworth Pastoral Press
An Imprint of The Haworth Press, Inc.

Hidden Addictions

A Pastoral Response to the Abuse of Legal Drugs

THE HAWORTH PASTORAL PRESS
Pastoral Care, Ministry, and Spirituality
Richard Dayringer, ThD
Senior Editor

New, Recent, and Forthcoming Titles:

A Memoir of a Pastoral Counseling Practice by Robert L. Menz

When Life Meets Death: Stories of Death and Dying, Truth and Courage by Thomas W. Shane

The Heart of Pastoral Counseling: Healing Through Relationship, Revised Edition by Richard Dayringer

The Eight Masks of Men: A Practical Guide in Spiritual Growth for Men of the Christian Faith by Frederick G. Grosse

Hidden Addictions: A Pastoral Response to the Abuse of Legal Drugs by Bridget Clare McKeever

Hidden Addictions
A Pastoral Response
to the Abuse of Legal Drugs

Bridget Clare McKeever, SSL, PhD

The Haworth Pastoral Press
An Imprint of The Haworth Press, Inc.
New York • London

Published by

The Haworth Pastoral Press, an imprint of The Haworth Press, Inc., 10 Alice Street, Binghamton, NY 13904-1580

Cover design by Monica Seifert.

Library of Congress Cataloging-in-Publication Data

McKeever, Bridget Clare.
    Hidden addictions : a pastoral response to the abuse of legal drugs / Bridget Clare McKeever.
        p. cm.
    Originally presented as the author's thesis (PhD)
    Includes bibliographical references and index.
    ISBN 0-7890-0267-1 (alk. paper)
    1. Church work with medication abusers—United States. 2. Medication abuse—Religious aspects—Christianity. I. Title.
BV4460.4.M37 1998
261.8'32299—dc21
                                              97-37002
                                                CIP

To Howard J. Clinebell,
whose mentoring and support
encouraged me to write this book

ABOUT THE AUTHOR

Sister Bridget Clare McKeever, SSL, PhD, is Director of The Spirituality Center for the Catholic Diocese of Salt Lake City. She is also a member of the Sisters of St. Louis, an international religious institute with a region in California. A native of County Antrim, Ireland, and a U.S. resident since 1952, she is a pastoral counselor, spiritual director, and holds memberships in the American Association of Pastoral Counselors and Spiritual Directors International.

CONTENTS

Foreword

Pause and imagine that there is a hidden epidemic of drug dependency that causes more Americans to die or be injured than all illegal drugs combined. If this were true, treating and preventing such an addictive epidemic would be given high priority among our society's crucial health issues. Leaders in churches and society would share an urgent concern. In this valuable book, Bridget Clare McKeever provides carefully documented evidence that such an epidemic does, in fact, exist. It consists of addictions to and dependency on prescribed and over-the-counter drugs.

These addictions and dependencies are sneaky, often developing gradually so that neither the victims nor their families are aware of the creeping entrapment process. Because it is legal drugs, including those prescribed by respected physicians, which are being abused, these addictions and dependencies do not push people's warning buttons until they are far advanced. Because it is hidden and polite, this form of drug abuse is probably highly prevalent among church members. This means that pastoral caregivers often have strategic opportunities to prevent such polite drug abuse by effective education. In addition, caregivers who know the danger signs may help possible victims recognize the nature of their problem and accept referral to appropriate therapies.

Dr. McKeever overviews both current understanding of these drug dependencies and methods for helping those affected by them. She summarizes succinctly the seven categories of legal drugs most often abused in our society. She highlights the special issues involved in dealing effectively with addiction to or dependency on legal drugs as contrasted with illegal drugs. She also summarizes the dynamics of prevalent dependencies within such highly vulnerable groups as women, youth, the aged, and the poor. The first three of these groups are well represented and in need in many congregations. The church's key role in prevention is described, with emphasis on two levels of such intervention: individual and social. Abundant case vignettes illuminate the discussion. In these ways, Dr. McKeever puts a wealth of useful information at the fingertips of pastoral caregivers, victims, and their families.

A major strength of the book is Dr. McKeever's keen awareness of the complex interaction of psychosocial, physiological, and spiritual causes of addictions and drug dependencies. With raised consciousness about the social context of the individual problems, she shows how sexist socialization of many women makes them acutely vulnerable to these addictions and dependencies. Furthermore, the sexism of many male physicians contributes to the reality that these drugs are prescribed twice as often to women as to men.

Another special strength of the book for pastoral caregivers is the author's expertise in spiritual direction and rituals, as these relate to treating addictions and dependencies. She shows how spiritual and social pathologies in the churches—including sexist theologies that reinforce attitudes in some male clergy—stimulate the creeping dependency process in some women. These same pathologies serve the destructive function of keeping the problem hidden—from the victims, their families, and from caregiving professionals, including clergy. It is crucial that the near silence of churches about this form of drug abuse be replaced by its open recognition and discussion. Until this happens, it is unlikely that pastoral caregivers will initiate appropriate treatment of effective prevention on the comprehensive scale that is needed.

The author of this book has an in-depth knowledge of the issues, derived from research done originally for her PhD dissertation. Here the gist of what caregivers need to know is presented in nontechnical and nonacademic terms. Bridget Clare McKeever has illuminated the downside of the marvel-producing "age of psychochemistry" that has brought humankind so many "wonder drugs" for treating human distress and diseases.

As a person with a long interest in understanding and treating addictions, I am pleased to be able to recommend this innovative book wholeheartedly! I predict that it will be a useful blessing to pastoral caregivers as well as to the many lonely and confused individuals and families in congregations who are on the slippery slope of legal drug addiction and dependency.

Howard J. Clinebell Jr.

Preface

In 1978, when Barbara Gordon's autobiography *I'm Dancing As Fast As I Can* was published, little was known about addiction to prescription drugs. Gradually, however, other women began to see their own agonies reflected in Ms. Gordon's. In the same year, Betty Ford's autobiography *The Times of My Life* alerted the public to the problem of dependency on painkillers and the particular hazards of combining prescription drugs with alcohol. Consciousness regarding the indiscriminate prescribing of tranquilizers was heightened by Hughes and Brewin's *The Tranquilizing of America* in 1979. Then came Nellis's *The Female Fix* in 1989, and the problem of the abuse of prescription drugs was fully out of the closet.

As the decade of the 1980s wore on, however, publicity on the abuse of cocaine began to turn attention to that drug. This was an illegal drug; it was being abused by all classes. As well as generating a lucrative black market, it was reportedly causing other crimes: violence, prostitution to support the habit, and more. Gradually concern about the abuse of legal drugs diminished. Now, in the second half of the 1990s, except for occasional reports on the abuse of steroids by athletes, one seldom sees anything new written or reported on the abuse of prescription and over-the-counter (OTC) drugs. Nevertheless, sedatives, painkillers, sleeping pills, diet pills, laxatives, and other OTC drugs, as well as steroids, are being abused in homes, schools, locker rooms, and nursing homes by thousands of women, girls, elders, men, and boys. The cost in terms of diminished health, reduction in the quality of human life, and in human productivity is immense.

Because abuse of legal drugs is, for the most part, a hidden problem, pastoral caregivers have a heightened opportunity and obligation to respond pastorally. They are, as professionals, in a good position to do so because they are less likely than persons in the medical or psychiatric field to have a stake in denying it. They do not benefit financially from the sale of pharmaceutical drugs, they receive no perks from pharmaceutical companies. Moreover, they are, by profession, dedicated to an ethical stance that places the good of individuals and society above every other consideration. This commitment means that they should be constantly on the lookout for problems that are not receiving attention from the culture or from others in the helping professions. The purpose of this book is to give guidance to pastoral caregivers to detect possible abuse of prescription and over-the-counter drugs and to help those who suffer from this malady.

Although psychotropic drugs have diminished human suffering and have brought healing to many, they have also been abused by both prescribers and recipients. Because there is considerable lack of awareness of this problem, Chapter 1 indicates its nature and extent. Chapter 2 describes the legal drugs that are most frequently abused, the dynamics of addiction, and the vulnerable populations.

Drug abuse is both a symptom and an autonomous disorder. As a symptom it is a reaction to what Anne Wilson Schaef calls "The Addictive Society." Chapter 3 examines this sociocultural context, in which abuse of prescription and OTC drugs occur. This chapter is based on Schaef's thesis that Western culture is fundamentally addicted to power and control on the one hand and compliancy and subservience on the other. All other addictions and dependencies are ways of coping with these two fundamental addictions. Secondary addictions and dependencies, once established, take on a life of their own. They must be treated first; however, eliminating the primary cause will not automatically cure what Schaef designates the primary addiction.

Both the fundamental dependency of society and the secondary addictions and dependencies of individuals have a spiritual basis. They are a misguided and destructive attempt to overcome the anxiety generated by the tension between radical human limitation and human yearning for the infinite. Chapter 4 elaborates on the spiritual implications of drug abuse.

Chapter 5 describes a pastoral response to prescription and OTC drug abuse in the individual and the family. It indicates that this disorder requires a holistic approach and multifaceted treatment. Pastoral caregivers, depending on opportunity and training, may enter the treatment process at various times and contribute in various ways, from initial intervention to prevention.

Chapter 6 addresses the underlying societal disorder and delineates various ways in which pastoral persons may, by working toward systemic change, seek to prevent abuse of prescribed and OTC drugs.

Acknowledgments

Many books have a long gestation period. This one is no exception. I first became interested in the problem of substance abuse when, in 1979, I took a course in alcoholism with Professor Howard Clinebell at the School of Theology at Claremont, California. In the summer of 1980 I did a unit of Clinical Pastoral Education (CPE) in Pomona Valley Community Hospital, Pomona, California. It was there that I came in contact for the first time with patients addicted to Valium. I learned much from these patients, from Dr. Vickie Fox, MD, and from Chaplain James Rhoades about what was then a relatively new disorder. This experience generated in me an ongoing interest in what is still a hidden addiction and led me to write my doctoral dissertation on dependency on prescribed drugs in women. During that time I also came to know Dr. Charlotte Ellen, an activist in the women's movement of the 1980s. From her I learned to examine critically women's place in society and its many subsystems. Her influence remains with me to this day.

Though they were not involved directly in the genesis of this book, Professor Carmel McEnroy, RSM, Lexington Theological Seminary, and Professor Damian Dietlein, OSB, St. Meinrad School of Theology, lent support through their friendship. I am grateful to all of these persons. Finally, I thank in particular my religious community, the Sisters of St. Louis, for granting me a sabbatical during which this book was written.

Chapter 1

The Problem

Delma does not remember her husband's funeral. She remembers the police at the door telling her about the accident, hearing herself screaming, her son calling the family doctor for a sedative, and after that a blur of numbed pain. In fact, the past ten years during which she met, married, and divorced her second husband; parented a stepdaughter from age eight to age sixteen; babysat her grandchildren; and finally overdosed on Xanax have an unreal quality. She felt like a spectator in her own life, behind a shield that blunted but did not remove emotional pain, always struggling to drag herself day by day out of the quagmire of depression. She did not intend to kill herself when she took that overdose, only to end the agony which her life had become. Fortunately, she survived and found a better way to improve her life.

*   *   *

Guadalupe is sixteen; she is five-foot-four and weighs ninety-three pounds. That's four pounds heavier than when she was admitted to a center for the treatment of eating disorders. Her journey there began three years ago when, at a plump one-hundred-forty pounds, she failed to get a place on the cheerleading squad. Those chosen were all approximately a slim one-hundred-five pounds. For Guadalupe, the failure was the end of her world. She was smart, she was coordinated, her friends said she was cute, but she was just too fat. She stopped going out with her friends, her grades fell from Bs to Ds. She tried dieting, but food was her only comfort and after losing five pounds, she would give up and gain ten.

Guadalupe became more withdrawn; she began to tell her friends that she wished she were dead. In alarm her mother took her to a doctor who prescribed Prozac for her depression. The Prozac replaced her depression with bouts of anxiety and hyper-activity, but it had one great benefit. She stopped feeling hungry, she ate less and less, and the pounds dropped off. Life looked much better. Pleased with her progress, the doctor weaned her off the Prozac. Now her only problem was maintaining her weight loss. Remarking how skinny she looked, her mother began to urge her to eat more, and with her returning appetite, it was difficult for Guadalupe to resist. Then one day a friend confided to her the secret of her slim figure. She had a boyfriend who gave her pills that worked like a charm. She could get some for Gua-dalupe for a few dollars. Guadalupe felt a little guilty and scared about buying the pills, but her friend assured her that they were not illegal. "Lots of people get them from their doctors," she said. The pills were amphetamines. A year later and forty-five pounds lighter, Guadalupe was very happy with her high energy and her slim body—until she passed out after gym class and was taken to the hospital emergency unit. Two months later she was referred from a drug rehabilitation center to an eating disorder clinic.

* * *

The Johnson's have just returned from their son's funeral. They are heartbroken. He was their oldest son, a fine student, and a splendid athlete. When he collapsed and died on the football field, it was thought that he had succumbed to a hidden heart anomaly. The autopsy revealed that he had been taking large doses of steroids. The steroids, rather than exercise, created his magnificent physique. Now rumors are flying that a doctor had been supplying him and others on the college football squad. The parents are bitter and confused. They will sue the doctor and the college but that will not bring their son back.

* * *

Marcia is worried about her father. It was a difficult decision to have him placed in a nursing home. But she and her husband, Jim, both work outside the home, and since his stroke, her father could not be left alone for a long period. Moreover, he was becoming incontinent and needed more care than a housekeeper could give. After being admitted to the home, her father had been very angry. Each time she visited, he complained about everything and demanded to be taken home. Then, to her relief, the complaining stopped. He became quiet and amenable. He stopped asking to be taken home. However, for the past several days he seemed quite "out of it." He slept a lot, even nodding off in the middle of his dinner. Marcia asked the director about the change she had noticed and was told that her father was having difficulty sleeping and that he was given a sedative to help him adjust to the nursing home and to sleep. When she asked what her father was being given and how much, she was told that he was under good medical supervision and that she should trust the judgment of the medical personnel who were doing what was best for her father. Marcia was afraid to push the issue in case the nursing home would tell her to remove her father.

———————

Many people similar to those described above would not consider themselves addicts. In fact, some of them might even be vocal opponents to the legalizing of street drugs. They could be anyone's mother, sister, father, or brother. They could be this writer; they could be you, the reader. They are abusers of legal drugs. They are like people whom pastoral ministers meet in the ordinary course of their ministry. They are like many who attend church or synagogue regularly, belong to youth groups, or are star athletes at church-sponsored colleges. Persons like them suffering from their hidden malady may be receiving ongoing pastoral therapy for another presenting problem without the therapist being aware of their hidden addiction. It is important that pastoral caregivers become aware of the nature and extent of this problem because often, if they only knew, they would be in a prime position to help.

PREVALENCE OF LEGAL DRUG ABUSE

According to a 1982 report issued by the United States General Accounting Office, more Americans die or are injured from the abuse of prescription drugs than from the use of all illegal drugs combined.[1] The Drug Abuse Warning Network claims that 60 percent of all drug-related emergency room visits and 70 percent of all drug-related deaths involve prescription drugs. A report from the United States Health and Human Services indicates that more than half of the fatalities from drug reactions are persons over sixty years of age. Some studies have shown that 90 percent of the elderly suffer drug side effects from the improper use of prescription and over-the- counter drugs and that 20 percent of them required hospitalization as a result. One of every twenty persons living in a nursing home has drug-induced senility, according to the National Institute on Aging.[2] Data reported by the Drug Abuse Warning Network indicate that, in 1987, fourteen of the twenty most common causes of drug overdose, dependence, or other adverse effects were caused by either prescription or over-the-counter drugs.[3]

PERSONS MOST AT RISK

For most people, the term "drug abuser" is associated with street junkies strung out on narcotics, pushers selling crack in inner city alleys, and amateur chemists brewing freebase in empty tenements. Their imagination may even stretch to include college students smoking pot in the fraternity and sorority houses, or to professionals discretely snorting cocaine in their offices between appointments and after office hours. Few associate the term with persons who buy their drugs at the local pharmacy or supermarket or take them from the family medicine cabinet. Even fewer think of over-the-counter medicines as possible substances of abuse. Milton Silverman and Philip Lee recount in *Pills, Profits, and Politics* how a patient warned by her doctor to take no drugs or medicines other that what had been prescribed continued to take large amounts of aspirin on the assumption that it was not a medicine because she could buy it at the corner grocery store.[4]

Elizabeth Lambert of NIDA's Division of Epidemiology and Prevention Research presented the following findings at the National Symposium on Medicine and Public Policy. Sixteen percent of persons in the United States aged twelve years and over have abused at least one prescription drug during their lifetime. Of these, 27 percent of persons between ages twenty-six and thirty-four were found to have abused prescribed drugs. As Lambert says, "Any kind of drug abuse should cause alarm, but when drugs are acquired legally, people may feel more at liberty to use them."[5] Studies made in 1990 indicated that approximately 7 percent of male high school students have tried steroids and that 20 percent of high school football players use them. An estimated 17 to 20 percent of college athletes are users. These percentages represent a total of approximately one million students.[6]

Though anyone is liable to abuse legal drugs, some segments of the population are more vulnerable than others. These are youth, both female and male; women; and the elderly. It is important that pastoral caregivers be specially aware of the risk of abuse among these populations.

Girls and Young Women

Because of the cultural association between slimness and beauty, the abuse of diet pills is a major hazard for girls. A survey of drug use among high school seniors found that three times as many women used diet pills as men. Half of all female seniors reported using them in the past year. Amphetamines are still being prescribed for the treatment of obesity, though that use has decreased over the past several years. However, products sold in health food stores, drugstores, or weight reduction clinics lure the teen girl with the promise of a speedy reduction of weight and a svelte body. Pills made from the amino acids arginine and ornithine claim to stimulate human growth hormone. If the claim is true, then they may also stimulate other hormones and alter insulin levels and carbohydrate metabolism. Fad diets, pills, and potions may create more problems than they solve.[7] Another hazard of the abuse of diet pills among young women is that they may become the prelude to eating disorders such as anorexia and bulimia.

Boys and Young Men

Whereas diet pills are the legal drug most likely to be abused by young females, steroids are frequently the licit drug of choice for young males. Being thin is the cultural ideal for females; being muscular is the ideal for males. Though some obtain steroids and information about them from physicians, the majority obtain them from fellow athletes, bodybuilders, through mail order catalogues, or from gyms. In these cases when an adverse reaction occurs, or when users incur physical damage through long-term use, they are less likely to have access to physicians who might detect problems and intervene.[8]

Older Women

Probably the group most at risk from the abuse of prescribed drugs are middle-aged women. In the late 1970s The National

Institute on Drug Abuse (NIDA) statistics claimed that 60 percent of all drug-related emergency room visits were made by women. Two-thirds of these cases were suicide attempts; the remainder needed treatment because of dependence on mind-altering drugs. It was estimated that doctors wrote 90 million prescriptions annually. Most of them were written for women. NIDA estimated that there were in the United States between one and two million women who abused medication and who subsequently became dependent on these drugs.[9] Demographics of benzodiazepine users and abusers in 1980 indicated 64 percent female to 36 percent male.[10] Annabel Hecht noted that although a small number of women procured their drug supplies from the street, most of them did not resemble and did not identify with "street junkies." They were housewives, working mothers, college students, single parents, professionals. They cut across socioeconomic lines to include the affluent and those on welfare, ranging from a first lady to a destitute single parent.[11] The findings of a Texas study made in 1986 suggest that women over forty are a particularly high-risk group.[12]

It may be argued that these statistics reflect the decades when the public was having its romance with minor tranquilizers. When they were first marketed, Valium, Librium, and other benzodiazepines were thought to be safe for the treatment of anxiety and were recommended by the pharmaceutical industry and prescribed widely by physicians for even the normal tensions of life. Since the mid-1980s the dangers of prescribing these drugs indiscriminately and their potential for abuse have been well documented and are better appreciated by the general public. Several states have made moves to control the inappropriate prescribing of benzodiazepines. As a result there has been a decline in the number of minor tranquilizer prescriptions written. However, Xanax, a benzodiazepine, was ranked seventh in the number of prescriptions written between July 1992 and June 1993.[13] Moreover, researchers Michael Weintraub and colleagues who studied the effect of regulatory laws in New York State note the following:

> The main negative impact of the regulations measured to date has been increase in prescriptions for alternative medications. The alternative sedative-hypnotic medications are less effective, more likely to be abused, and more dangerous in overdose than benzodiazepines.[14]

It seems unwarranted, therefore, to conclude that the decline in the number of tranquilizer prescriptions indicates a corresponding decline in the numbers of women who use and abuse prescription drugs in the 1990s. This author has noted the scarcity of data on women and prescription drug abuse since the late 1980s. This phenomenon may indicate that the issue has gone into remission in public interest and as a popular topic for research—a situation which should be more alarming than reassuring.

Elders

It is estimated that twenty-five percent of all prescription drugs are written for persons over sixty-five years of age. However, these elderly comprise only 11 percent of the population. In one regional psychiatric hospital, 65 percent of the older adult admissions were related to medication abuse and misuse. Some studies have found that 90 percent of the elderly have suffered from the side effects of medicine and, of these, 20 percent required hospitalization. Older adults use over-the-counter drugs frequently. In Michigan a survey found that half the seniors interviewed used over-the-counter pain relievers, laxatives, and/or antacids four or five times a week.[15]

Not only are the elderly in jeopardy because of the quantity of medication they take, they are also liable to have adverse side effects because of physiological changes associated with aging. The distribution and elimination of drugs is slowed down in the system in the elderly. For this reason older adults may need lower dosages than those required for younger persons. However, because the FDA does not require testing to determine the correct dosage for the elderly, standard dosages may often be prescribed. Older adults may also be abusing alcohol and using it in combination with medication, making them more at risk of overdose. Elders whose memories are failing and who self-medicate are also in danger of overmedicating accidentally.

According to Robert B. Sause, RPh, of St. John's University College Pharmacy in Jamaica, New York, 40 to 60 percent of elders use at least one OTC drug daily.[16] Apparently, the very old and the very poor self-medicate more than any other group. While there are benefits that OTC's offer the elderly, there are also significant risks. The elderly may misread OTC labels (the print is usually very small) and take medications that are not appropriate for their symptoms or that may interact negatively with other medications they are taking. When previous prescription drugs are switched to OTC, there is an illusion that they are now completely safe. This is not the case, and they often pose a high risk for adverse drug interaction for elders who are also taking prescribed drugs. Frederick Mayer, the president of Pharmacists Planning Service, Inc., Sausalito, California, cites studies which indicate that 240,000 Americans are hospitalized annually because of drug interactions. Of these, 100,000 will die.[17]

Another negative effect of the misuse and abuse of drugs by the elderly is the prevalence of injurious falls. About 33 percent of persons over sixty-five years fall at least once each year, and of these, over 40 to 60 percent sustain injuries. Injuries are the fifth most common cause of death in elderly populations.[18] A study by Keijo Koski and colleagues. indicates that injurious falls by male elders result from a combination of physiological factors associated with aging, and the use of such drugs as long-acting benzodiazepines, digitalis glycosides, calcium blockers, and anti-inflammatory drugs. In female elders such falls were associated with the use of long-acting benzodiazepines, calcium blockers, and some drugs used to improve peripheral circulation.[19]

Special Populations

As well as the above groups, there are indications that other segments of the population not distinguished by age or gender may have a proclivity for the abuse of legal drugs. Some studies have indicated a possible link between the use of illicit drugs and requests for psychotherapeutic medication initiated by patients. A survey conducted by the National Institute of Mental Health in 1981 clearly indicated such a relationship. In this study, 1,716 persons aged eighteen to forty-four were interviewed. Thirty-two percent had used illicit drugs, 39 percent had used psychotherapeutic medicine, and 46 percent had psychiatric symptoms. The link was not explained by the incidence of psychiatric symptoms. It was hypothesized that the association between the use of illicit drugs and prescribed drugs might be related to learned behavior or sensation-seeking behavior theory. This study gives reason to suspect that persons who have used illicit drugs during adolescence may seek prescription drugs in adulthood, perceiving them to be a more mature option.[20]

Though there are no validating studies, anecdotal evidence seems to indicate that persons of either gender who suffer from a psychiatric disorder for which they are taking psychotropic drugs and who are not adequately supervised are liable to abuse these drugs. Some may overdose intentionally. Others may take them sporadically, or may cease abruptly when they become discouraged with their effectiveness, or when they experience a marked improvement in their condition.

Finally, in recent years concern has been growing regarding legal substance abuse by children. Some medications and volatile substances can be purchased by almost anyone. Among these are glue and cough syrup. Children of grade school age have been known to seek a high by sniffing glue, paint thinner, or the gas used in aerosol cans, a most dangerous habit that can cause brain damage. They are also liable to ingest large quantities of cough syrup, which contains a morphine-like drug. The fact that many children spend after-school hours unsupervised provides opportunity for dangerous experimentation with these and similar substances.[21]

Not only is it important that pastoral caregivers and other pastoral ministers are aware of populations who are vulnerable to legal drug abuse, it is also necessary that they know something of the types of drugs abused, their effects, the major forms of abuse, and the dynamics of addiction. These are the subject of the next chapter.

Chapter 2

Pills, People, and Process

It is not the purpose of this author to condemn the use of drugs. Many diseases have been eliminated or arrested through their use. We may well owe an increase in the quality and length of life to the judicious use of drugs. What is of concern here is the abuse and misuse of drugs. Though I will discuss mainly drug abuse and a pastoral response to this disorder, I will also devote some space to a discussion of drug misuse. For the sake of clarity I wish to explain how I will use the following terms throughout this book: *abuse, misuse, addiction, dependency.*

By *abuse* I mean the compulsive, destructive, or inappropriate use (or prescribing) of psychoactive substances such as Valium, Xanax, Klonopin, Dalmane, codeine, Halcion, Prozac, various steroids, and over-the-counter drugs such as sleeping aids, pain killers, diuretics, laxatives, and diet pills. There are a number of ways in which drugs are abused. They may be prescribed for life problems for which they provide no lasting remedy or simply to make patients easier to handle by staff in hospitals or nursing homes. They may be taken intentionally in excess of the recommended dosage or combined with alcohol or other dugs in order to produce a heightened effect. They may be taken for purposes for which they are not intended. They may be taken when they are no longer therapeutic simply in order to feed a physical or emotional addiction. Drug abuse, as I understand it, is intentional, though not always subject to the abuser's control; even addicted abusers know that they are abusing substances athough they may have lost control over their behavior.

The *misuse* of drugs, on the other hand, is unintentional, the result of misinformation, ignorance, confusion, or lapse of memory. Many people simply do not understand the dangers of mixing drugs; for example, of taking prescribed medication in combination with some over-the-counter drugs or with certain foods or with alcohol. The elderly, many of whom have to take several pills each day, may forget what they have taken and accidentally overdose or underdose, or may abruptly stop taking a drug that should be terminated gradually.

The term *addiction* is meant to describe a condition in which a person has developed a severe physical need for a drug. If he or she does not take it, withdrawal will set in. Usually tolerance accompanies addiction. (See the section Dynamics of Addiction and Dependency for further explanation of tolerance.)

I will use the term *dependence* to refer to the compulsive need of a substance for psychological and/or social reasons. Unlike addiction, dependence does not involve withdrawal or physical craving. It is possible for a person who is addicted to a drug to also experience emotional, psychological, or social dependence on it. A sign of emotional dependence would be a marked change in mood when the drug is discontinued. Psychological dependence is marked by the inability to cope with ordinary life problems without the drug. Social dependence involves the need to indulge in the drug in order to be socially accepted.

The scenarios described at the beginning of Chapter 1 represent sections of the population that are most vulnerable to the abuse or misuse of legal drugs: women, teens, and the elderly. In order to understand legal drug abuse better, we will first examine the kinds of drugs most frequently abused. Then we will discuss the nature and dynamics of drug abuse.

LEGAL DRUGS OF ABUSE

Legal drugs that are liable to be abused fall into seven categories: tranquilizers, sedatives, antidepressants, stimulants and other diet pills, pain killers, steroids, and over-the-counter drugs.

Tranquilizers

Tranquilizers are classified as major or minor, depending not on their potency, but on their use. The major tranquilizers such as Stelazine, Thorazine, and Reserpine are used with psychotic patients both in hospital and in outpatient programs. They tend to suppress bodily reactions to emotional states, such as aggressiveness and anxiety, and make the patient more amenable to therapy. Although the major tranquilizers can be abused, especially when they are utilized to suppress symptoms which remain untreated, they are not readily available to the average person suffering from "normal" anxiety and, therefore, are not likely to be the drug of choice of a dependent person.

Minor tranquilizers, which include Librium, Valium, Klonopin, Atavan, Xanax, Dalmane, and Halcion, are prescribed for less serious emotional disorders marked by anxiety, tension, and irrational fears. They are also used as muscle relaxants. In some people they may produce a sense of well-being and euphoria. Because almost everyone suffers at some time from anxiety, minor tranquilizers are sought much more often than major tranquilizers. For this reason as well as because of the properties of the drugs themselves, they lend themselves to abuse and are conducive to dependence.

Frequent and heavy use can produce symptoms such as dizziness, low blood pressure, drowsiness, and depression, symptoms that may be interpreted as the result of emotional states and as warranting increased doses of the culprit drug. A number of minor tranquilizers have been found to be capable of producing physical dependence and of serious withdrawal symptoms if taken in high dosages over an extended period of time. Abrupt cessation of these drugs can result in severe depression, disorientation, agitation, illusions, hallucinations, and even convulsions.[1] In the event of long-term use, many of these drugs remain in the system for several weeks after the patient has discontinued use; therefore, withdrawal symptoms may not be experienced for some time. The patient, and sometimes even the physician, may ascribe the withdrawal symptoms to emotional causes and resume taking or prescribing the drug. These dynamics may set up a sequence of use, dependency, and abuse.

Sedatives

Sedatives are barbiturates that depress the central nervous system. They are of two kinds: slow starting types such as phenobarbital, Amytal, and butabarbital; and short-acting, fast-starting kinds such as Seconal, Nembutal, and secobarbital. This second type, because of its fast-acting effect, is more likely to be abused. Barbiturates have been used to relieve anxiety but they are prescribed mainly as sleeping pills. Misuse of sedatives produces symptoms similar to that of alcohol intoxication, marked by a staggering gate, slurred speech, impaired judgment, and emotional volatility. Withdrawal can result in convulsions, temporary psychosis, and even death. Convulsions may even occur during a period of decreased dosage.[2]

Recently, a sedative-hypnotic, Rohypnol (flunitrazepam), has received considerable media attention because of its association with date rape. Although this drug is not approved for marketing in the United States, it is easily obtained in Latin America, Europe, Asia, and Australia. Its medical uses are for preoperative sedation and as a treatment for insomnia. However, a field investigation conducted in south Texas gave some reason to believe that it—along with a variety of sedatives collectively classified by abusers as Roaches—is being obtained illegally by young persons including college students. Since 1989 the abuse of these drugs has been a matter of concern for law enforcement agencies. It appears that much of the flunitrazepam being abused is obtained in Mexico or smuggled into Florida from Latin American countries.

The Texas study indicated that Rohypnol is taken by young users as an intoxicant in combination with or instead of alcohol. A major danger of this drug is that it can have a disinhibiting effect which impairs judgment and may lead users to engage in dangerous behavior, including driving while intoxicated. It can also cause amnesia. Withdrawal symptoms include craving and anxiety. A disturbing finding in this study is that many of the youth interviewed had taken a variety of pills which they called Roaches and which were not Rohypnol. Apparently, they did not pay much attention to what they were taking.[3]

Antidepressants

Antidepressants fall into three categories: tricyclic, monoamine oxidase inhibitors (MOIs), and mixtypes. Antidepressants are prescribed for long-term mood disorders that are understood to result from a physical chemical imbalance. Examples of antidepressants include the following: Tofranil, Elavil, Pamelor, Vivactil (tricyclics); Marplan, Nardil, Parnate, Eudonyl (MOIs); Ludiomil, Wellbutrin, Desyrel, and Prozac (mixtypes). MOIs are particularly dangerous when mixed with other substances (chocolate, aged cheese, hard liquor) or with other antidepressants.

Antidepressants may be misused by being prescribed for or used by persons whose depression is a healthy reaction to an oppressive situation, or to the ordinary ups and downs of life. Because many of these drugs have been on the market for a short time only, the effects of long-term use are not known.[4] Antidepressants are slow-acting, thus they are less likely to be abused by addicts. However, they have side effects that need to be carefully weighed against their benefits.

Painkillers

Many prescribed pain relievers, such as Darvon, Demerol, and Percodan, as well as medicines containing codeine are narcotics. They act on the central nervous system with analgesic effects and are therapeutically the most effective pain relievers. They have other effects such as drowsiness or sedation, respiratory depression, and mood changes. If misused, such opiate drugs have serious effects including tolerance, physical dependency, and psychological dependency which can produce withdrawal symptoms even before physical dependence has occurred. If dependence has developed, and the supply of the narcotic is cut off, symptoms occur. These vary with the degree of physical dependence that has been established. Withdrawal symptoms may include restlessness, insomnia, shivering, irritability, muscular tremors, vomiting, and diarrhea.[5]

Stimulants

Stimulants such as benzedrine, hexedrine, and methedrine have been in use in medical practice for about thirty-five years. Their main use has been to control narcolepsy, to relieve fatigue in persons suffering from psychomotor impairment, to treat mild depression, to control appetite, to counteract depressant drugs, and to enhance the action of analgesic drugs. Amphetamines are the stimulants most liable to abuse. Currently the prescription of amphetamines is restricted to cases of narcolepsy, hyperkinesia (in children), and weight reduction. Some states have imposed restrictions on the use of amphetamines for weight control.[6] However, there are other hazardous drugs that can be purchased over the counter by teens anxious to speed their development and alleviate growing pains. Some of these are downright fraudulent and are merely worthless, but others are dangerous. The active ingredient in most nonprescription diet pills is either phenylpropanolamine or benzocaine. Too much of the former can cause elevated blood pressure. Benzocaine is supposed to work by numbing the inside of the mouth so as to make food less satisfying. Depending on their composition, some diet pills can cause nervousness, nausea, and insomnia. They can also be addictive.[7]

In 1996, the FDA approved Redux (dexfenfluramine) for the management of obesity. This drug should be used in addition to a reduced caloric diet and a regime of exercise, and only under strict medical supervision. Redux seems to increase serotonin levels, which are associated with the control of appetite. It has been found to have such adverse effects as diarrhea, dry mouth, and somnolence. A study made on rats showed that high doses of dexfenfluramine produced neurochemical changes in their brains.[8] Although Redux is only recommended for persons who have serious obesity problems, to be used in conjunction with exercise and healthy diet, it is likely that it will fall into the hands of persons for whom it has not been prescribed and who do not need it for the treatment of obesity.

Anabolic Steroids

Anabolic steroids are another product that appeals to the teen's and young adult's preoccupation with body image. These are compounds similar to the male hormone testosterone. They are used appropriately to treat delayed puberty in adolescents, anemia, and severe burns. They are abused by both boys and girls, but more frequently by boys. They may be used by athletes to build muscle, but are also used by young men who are not athletic merely to enhance their appearance. According to experts on the subject, they are also used in combination with weight-lifting programs by law enforcement officers in order to make themselves look more threatening to criminals. Actually, steroids do not build muscle without concomitant exercise. Moreover, the advantage in muscle buildup is seriously offset by the side effects of the prolonged use of these drugs. Steroid use can cause liver tumors, jaundice, heart and blood disorders, sterility, and the masculinization of female fetuses in pregnant women. It was noted in the *Journal of the American Medical Association*, January 20, 1987 that the use of steroids "may expose athletes to the risk of injury to ligaments and tendons and that these injuries take longer to heal."[9] In February 1991, anabolic steroids were placed on Schedule III of the Controlled Substances Act. This means that no one may manufacture, distribute, or dispense them without registration from the DEA. Nevertheless, athletes can still obtain these drugs illegally from bodybuilders, gyms, via mail order, and on the black market.[10]

Over-the-Counter Drugs

Practically all over-the-counter drugs are potential drugs of abuse or misuse: laxatives, sleeping pills, cough medicines, cold remedies, diet pills, antacids. OTCs may be ingested in large numbers in order to heighten their effect or may be taken in combination with alcohol. They may be used in suicide attempts. Silverman and Lee point out that self-treatment with OTCs over a long period of time may be very dangerous. Persons may overdose "in the belief that if three pills do not work, then nine pills should work three times as well." Patients may take OTCs for months to remedy what turns out to be a fast-growing tumor.[11]

One major area of abuse is the practice of quackery. Teens and the aged are the main targets of quacks. An article "Quackery Targets Teens," in *FDA Consumer Magazine* points out that the young, in their impatience with the blossoming process, are fertile ground for quacks. "Teenagers are ready to experiment with products that promise to speed their growth development and ease their growing pains." In one-parent and two-working-parent families, teenagers often do the grocery shopping and consequently have access to their parents' credit cards or blank checks. They have ample opportunity to purchase whatever is available, from "space age diets" that "allow you to eat all day and still lose weight," to tanning pills and hair growth or removal lotions. Many of these are merely a waste of money but harmless; others, however, such as tanning pills containing color additives not approved by the FDA, can be harmful. Many quick loss diets and diet pills, which have side effects such as malnutrition, nausea, and insomnia, constitute health hazards.[12]

In addition, as early as the 1950s there was concern about the abuse of cough syrups by the young. At that time antitussives contained codeine or codeine-like compounds which, being available over-the-counter to anyone without regard to age, had high potential for abuse. However, until the 1990s the basis for concern about abuse was mainly anecdotal. In 1990 a survey of school personnel in the Waynesboro (Pennsylvania) School District was conducted in order to assess the degree of concern about the abuse of cough syrups among grade school and high school students. The results indicated that a majority of the school personnel considered the abuse of cough syrup and other OTC drugs to be increasing and to be a social problem among children and teens.[13] Although this study is preliminary and far from conclusive, it does indicate the need for further studies of this problem.

Over-the-counter medications which affect the digestive process are another group frequently abused. Laxatives are the drug of choice of young bulimics caught in the "binge and purge" cycle. They are also likely to be overused by elders who suffer from chronic constipation and who self-medicate without consulting their doctors. Antacids, similar to laxatives, are usually considered safe but they are frequently used to counteract the effects of nonsteroid anti-inflammatory drugs prescribed for arthritis. A study reported in the *Archives of Internal Medicine* (1996) indicates that antacids do not prevent gastrointestinal (GI) side effects. They have, however, been found to mask GI symptoms until the problem was so advanced as to require hospitalization.[14]

Look-Alike Drugs

A little-known mode of exploitation of the young is the manufacture and dissemination of "look-alike drugs." These may be purchased through mail-order catalogues. These drugs are intentionally made to look like amphetamines, barbiturates, or illegal street drugs. An issue of *FDA Consumer Magazine* says this about such fake drugs:

> These look-alikes generally contain decongestants, caffeine and other stimulants in what the FDA has called "dangerous illogical combinations." Some contain alarmingly high doses of one ingredient. When taken in excess or mixed with alcohol, the look-alikes have caused strokes and death. They are extremely dangerous when mixed with, or replaced by real "uppers" or "downers."[15]

DYNAMICS OF ADDICTION AND DEPENDENCY

Addiction is the condition in which a substance, which has ceased to alleviate the pain or discomfort for which it was originally taken, is experienced as necessary for one's well-being or even for survival. One is impelled to ingest the substance because the pain or discomfort of withdrawal and subsequent craving, which result from not indulging, seems greater than the negative consequence of indulging. One may also become psychologically dependent on a substance without experiencing physical craving or withdrawal. In this case, the person is convinced that he or she cannot cope with emotional pain or measure up to expectations without the drug. For example, a person may find that a particular drug alleviates physical pain or anxiety or seems to provide a short route to a desired physical condition such as slimness or a muscular physique. Even though the drug may be causing physical harm the person may feel impelled to continue using it.

In the case of diet pills and steroids, the abuser becomes increasingly convinced that they are necessary for social acceptance or for athletic prowess. This conviction will be maintained while the damage done by these drugs is denied. One can, of course, become dependent on certain behaviors such as gambling or exercising. These are not, however, the subject of this book.

Drug and Person Interaction

Many experts in the treatment of addiction consider the basic syndrome to be the same regardless of which chemical is abused. Vernelle Fox says:

> The principles of addiction are quite simple. Pain + relief = dependency. This is a basic phenomenon common to all of us. No problem, as long as it is simple physical hunger that is being fed. . . .[16]

However, while it would seem that the principles of addiction are similar regardless of the addicting substance, there are some factors associated with addiction to legal drugs which are unique to that particular form of addiction and to the populations involved.

The process of addiction is related to properties of the chosen drug interacting with characteristics of the person. Drugs vary in the rate at which they are secreted from the body. The amount of time it takes half the original level of a drug to leave the user's system is known as the half-life of the drug. Alcohol has a relatively short half-life; for example, the body will usually metabolize the alcohol in a can of beer in about two hours. Other drugs, however, have a relatively long half-life. Valium is reported to have a half-life of thirty to sixty hours. The half-life of a drug is also affected by another quality of potentially addictive drugs—tolerance. Tolerance means that the body quickly adjusts to a particular dosage of a drug so that, to obtain the same effect, the initial dosage has to be increased. Soon the body becomes accustomed to the higher dosage, which then has to be increased further to be effective.[17] The degree of tolerance is likely to vary from person to person.

Another phenomenon related to tolerance is the paradoxical effect of most mind-altering drugs. This effect means that when the drug wears off, the person does not return to the original premedicated state, but to a level of more acute distress—more depressed or more anxious. Thus, in addition to the need for a higher dosage because of physiological tolerance, there is psychological need for a higher dose because the person's symptoms have become aggravated by the supposed remedy. The person becomes caught in a cycle of rapidly growing addiction to a substance that is becoming increasingly ineffective for the purpose for which it was first taken.

Yet another attribute of psychotropic drugs that makes their effect difficult to predict is their synergistic effect on one another. A woman addicted to Valium describes this phenomenon. She had been taking Valium but it had become less effective in alleviating her anxiety. One day she and her husband were dining in a restaurant. Wine was served but she refused it because she was on Valium. Then, as she relates, "He (her husband) said, 'Go ahead and take it, you'll feel more comfortable, more relaxed,' and did I ever. . . . I hadn't felt so relaxed, I don't think ever." Almost all drugs are potentiated when combined with alcohol. Several have a potentiating effect on one another, thereby adding to the risk of overdosing in the case of drug-dependent persons who, as their addiction becomes more acute and their judgment unreliable, tend to mix pills indiscriminately.

No doubt many of the drugs mentioned above have legitimate uses in the treatment of physical and psychic ills. However, the facility with which emphasis has been placed on their benefits while their hazards have been minimized or discounted has contributed to problems, the magnitude of which we are only beginning to appreciate. Even when we are dealing with the use (as opposed to the obvious abuse) of these drugs, there is sometimes a failure to weigh the benefit/risk factor with sufficient seriousness and knowledge. In particular, the benefit/risk factor has to be weighed with great caution when the patient is a pregnant woman. Myron Brenton warns: "The American Academy of Pediatrics has advised its members that no drug has been proven safe for the unborn child."[18]

Drugs ingested by pregnant women pass through the placenta and penetrate the fetal organs, including the brain, before returning to the mother's circulatory system. What may be a safe dosage for the mother may constitute a gross overdose for the small, vulnerable fetus. The hazards of several drugs for pregnant women are already well-known. Diethylstilbestrol (DES), a synthetic hormone prescribed during pregnancy, has been found to cause increased risk of cervical cancer in female offspring and to cause an increased risk of birth defects. Similar risks attend when women who use birth control pills conceive too soon after cessation of the use of this contraceptive. The use of minor tranquilizers such as Valium early in pregnancy increases the risk of cleft palate in the baby. One study suggests a link between the use of minor tranquilizers and such birth defects as heart diseases, mental retardation, and partial deafness. Other studies have shown that when women take low to medium dosages of Valium during later stages of pregnancy, significant levels of the drug remain in the baby from eight to ten days after birth, resulting in possible respiratory difficulties and sucking problems. Barbiturates, sometimes given to pregnant women for hypertension, can cause withdrawal symptoms in the newborn child.

Conventional wisdom and even some professionals ascribe addiction to the drugs themselves. True, certain toxic and addictive properties in drugs themselves make their use always, though in varying degrees, hazardous to the health of the user. It seems likely that properties of certain drugs may determine which one becomes the "drug of choice" of a specific addicted person. However, the degree to which drugs themselves are the *cause* of abuse and/or addiction is debatable. Howard Clinebell disagrees that the substance alone causes dependency. He maintains that, in the case of alcohol, the long-term use coupled with the need to increase intake in order to maintain a normal level of functioning is descriptive rather than explanatory of the etiology of alcoholism.[19] It would seem that this assertion would apply to other drugs as well. As Clinebell does in regard to alcoholism, this author favors a theory of multicausal factors in the etiology of dependency on prescribed and over-the-counter drugs. These factors will be discussed in the next chapter.

Chapter 3

Sociological Roots of Addiction

It is a truism among drug counselors and in treatment centers that once a person has become drug-dependent, the cause of the dependency is irrelevant in the early stages of treatment. It is certainly true that prolonged analysis of the causes of the disorder can be a substitute for really dealing with the addiction and, consequently, an impediment to recovery. However, knowing something of the cause can be helpful in preventative programs, and may be relevant to the type of therapy employed and in formulating a comprehensive recovery program.

A popular traditional understanding of the cause of addiction, and one which undergirded the temperance movement and prohibition, was that substances, such as alcohol, cause addiction. There is an apparent validity to this perception. A person who never takes drugs never becomes addicted to them. However, ascribing addiction to the properties of substances does not explain why some who use drugs become addicted and some do not. This phenomenon might lead one to conclude that there is something inherent in the chemistry of some people which when exposed to certain other chemicals causes addiction. There may be some validity in this theory. Research in the area of physiology and alcoholism indicates some physiological predisposition to alcohol addiction. The same may be true for other drugs.

However, a physiological explanation does not account for the fact that some people become psychologically dependent on alcohol and other drugs without evincing symptoms of physical addiction. Personality theorists, who favor a psychological explanation of addiction, speak of the addictive personality and seek to delineate its characteristics. However, it is unclear whether the personality characteristics which substance abusers seem to share are the cause or the result of their addictions.

Rather than start with the individual, I prefer to begin my examination of the problem of addiction and substance abuse with the system in which the troubled person is embedded—society itself. Before examining the sociocultural dimensions of the addiction, it is necessary to describe the cultural matrix of this addiction.

THE ADDICTIVE SOCIETY

As far back as 1968, Howard Clinebell stated that sociocultural factors seem to be of prime importance in the choice of alcoholism as a symptom.[1] Since then the sociocultural roots of not only addictions but of addiction itself has been unequivocally designated by Anne Wilson Schaef. In *When Society Becomes an Addict*, Schaef argues persuasively that the ground of all addiction is the radically dependent nature of society itself.[2]

The "Addictive System," according to Schaef, is the "White Male System." It is addictive because it is based on power and control; it is white male because it has been and still is run by white males. It is the predominate system in Western society. However, this system is cocreated by the "Reactive Female System." The "Addictive System" might be said to be the child of the White Male/Reactive Female Systems. On the white male side the hallmarks are power and control; on the reactive female side they are powerlessness, subservience, and accommodation. Either side of this alliance can produce the symptom which Schaef terms "addiction."[3] Schaef defines addiction as " . . . any process over which we are powerless." She states, "It takes control over us, causing us to do and think things that are inconsistent with our values and leading us to become progressively more and more compulsive and obsessive."[4]

In light of Ms. Schaef's understanding of the addictive society, addiction or dependency on legal drugs are symptoms arising from the pervasive addictive society. They take their place among others in an increasing list of "addictive" disorders, such as alcoholism, workaholism, compulsive overeating, sexual addiction, and others, as a symptom of a pervasive addiction to power and control and their counterparts, powerlessness and nonliving. Even before Anne Wilson Schaef detected and named the connection between addiction and dependencies and the Addictive Society, insightful studies of female addicts were relating their disorder to sociocultural conditions. Beth Glover Reed, in *Treatment Services for Drug Dependent Women,* challenges the psychological profiles of drug-dependent women. She states that women who abuse drugs share many characteristics with one another and with women who are not drug-dependent. She says, "Many problems and issues that treatment of drug dependent women must address are related more to their being women than to their chemical dependency."[5] Reed comments on the consistent findings that women express lower levels of self-esteem and higher levels of depression and anxiety across all social classes. She cites the fact that women's and men's roles are not valued equally by society and that a large proportion of so-called masculine characteristics, such as competitiveness, are considered more "healthy" by a number of clinicians. She goes on to say that persons with lower social status internalize society's belief about them and hence feel less good about themselves and tend to orient themselves toward those who have more power. "Thus they devalue themselves and others like themselves. They have lower expectations of their lives, and tend to be more concerned about surviving and minimizing their discomfort than about getting ahead."[6]

Reed notes that "learned helplessness" resulting from physical and emotional abuse, accompanied by feelings of powerlessness, is also characteristic of drug-dependent women. The term "learned helplessness" was first used by M. E. Seligman who found that animals who are negatively reinforced, no matter what they do to try to escape a painful stimulus or to control a situation, stop trying in a relatively short time and rather than struggle to escape, will even succumb and die.[7] It is not surprising that a woman who sees no alternative other than to endure her situation may use drugs to minimize the distress, to survive, or in some cases, to commit suicide. Even when she may have alternatives, she may be so conditioned to hopelessness because of a history of powerlessness, she may be blind to them.

Althea is such a person. She had first been prescribed Valium after a miscarriage. It had, as she says, calmed her down, helped her to relax; it numbed her grief. This was a one-time use of the drug. However, a few years later, her husband, who was alcoholic, began to batter her. Living in a rural area, Althea was unacquainted with programs for abused spouses of alcoholic husbands. Even if she had been aware, she probably would not have availed of them. She was, as she says, "Too ashamed to tell anyone." When she consulted a doctor about her constant headaches (she explained the bruises as the result of falling down stairs), he diagnosed stress without asking her anything about what might be causing the headaches and prescribed Valium again. She was pleased because the Valium had helped her so much at the time of the miscarriage. The prescription read "Valium, 10 milligrams one or two times a day as needed." The Valium made her feel that everything was fine. "Take a pill and your troubles go away," she says wryly. Sometimes she would feel so good that she would stop taking the Valium. Soon, however, she would begin to feel very depressed and to have crying spells. Althea did not know enough about the drug she was taking to suspect withdrawal. She just resumed taking the Valium, now three times a day instead of two. It did not occur to her that she had any options regarding her marriage other than enduring with the help of Valium.

Frequently, women turn unacceptable feelings into depression. In general, societal expectations place more limitations on women than on men, especially in the area of sex and anger. In particular, expressions of anger and aggression are considered "unfeminine." Many women have considerable conflict and guilt about feeling angry and have developed few skills related to self-assertion. This seems particularly true of elderly women who grew up before the feminist movement. However, even some who are younger have so internalized the role ascribed to them by the culture that they have remained untouched by feminist ideologies. Homemaking and family-related roles (sometimes combined with that of assistant or only wage-earner) cause many women, including the drug-dependent, to feel that they have no option but to continue and endure their responsibilities. Even those who work outside the home may find themselves isolated in a predominantly male environment. This type of isolation is greatly aggravated for drug-dependent women. Such isolation prevents them from making a connection between the situation they are experiencing and broader social patterns. Hence, such women tend to blame themselves for situations they cannot change or control because they do not know that the problems they face are shared by many other women.

More women are working outside the home than ever before. This means that many, especially mothers who are separated, divorced, or unmarried, have the stress of part- or full-time work as well as child rearing. Add to that periods of unemployment (for underclass women), sexual harassment in the workplace, and conflict with former husbands over child support and/or custody, and we have a prescription for anxiety and depression. As Paula Nordstrom August says:

. . . . Rather than work on long-term solutions to their problems, some women turn to alcohol and tranquilizers as a means of coping with marital problems and the ongoing tribulations of motherhood. In this they are abetted by the medical establishment that too often dismisses female complaints with a prescription . . . when counseling and support are what is really needed.[8]

WOMEN AND THE MEDICAL PROFESSION

Another factor of significance in the use and abuse of psychotropic drugs is the attitude of physicians toward women. In recent decades, larger numbers of women have been entering medical school and going on to practice in various branches of medicine. Nevertheless, the overall medical establishment, especially its "hierarchy" is predominantly male. Heads of medical schools, their admissions directors, and those who teach students are predominantly male. Most practitioners are male. Yet the majority of patients are female. This means that the majority of women patients have male doctors.[9]

Ruth Cooperstock, a research scientist in the Addiction Research Foundation of Ontario, Canada, says, "Prior to any discussion of psychotropic drugs, it is necessary to recognize that these are products of a particular relationship, (that of) the patient to her or his doctor." Ms. Cooperstock points out that in the nineteenth century the American middle- and upper-class woman was considered "sickly" while working-class women were seen as sturdy and innately healthy. This mythology served the economic interest of the medical profession. Today, in spite of some changes in perception brought about through the feminist movement, there is still a mythology that connects women with neurosis and neurosis with stress. This view may be a basis for the high rate of psychotropic drug prescribing and use among women.

Needless to say, current mythology regarding women's illnesses serves the economic interests of the drug companies.[10]

In 1982, Myron Brenton quoted data which indicated the extent to which women are the major recipients of drug prescriptions. He stated that of the 121 million prescriptions doctors wrote annually in the early 1980s, twice as many went to women as to men. Though since then there has been a decline in tranquilizer prescriptions and in the number of medical emergencies caused by these drugs, the hazards of benzodiazepine abuse still persist.[11] There is still no evidence that the proportion cited by Brenton has changed significantly in the 1990s. Why is there such a preponderance of women receiving drug prescriptions? One reason is that women see doctors more frequently than men. Another factor is, as Cooperstock notes:

> . . . . women are less likely to deny their problem. They cope by seeking help from family, friends and clinics. Moreover, men tend to use alcohol to self-medicate, to externalize stress in aggressive behavior, or somatize it as heart and vascular problems.[12]

The situation of Althea mentioned earlier illustrates a well-recognized pattern. Her abusing husband eventually died of a heart attack. She became addicted to Valium.

The Medicalizing of Life Problems

The disease concept of alcoholism has been useful in alleviating the guilt of alcoholics and thereby has facilitated the recovery process. However, there is a distinct hazard in the contemporary tendency to universalize the medical model to include life problems. Ruth Cooperstock found, in a study of physician's perceptions of symptoms most frequently seen in their practice, that such problems as sleeplessness, general feelings of unhappiness, headache, and fatigue, as well as loneliness, financial difficulties, and problems with children are seen more commonly as female issues. She notes that when "problems of living" are presented in the physician's office, they are transformed into medical problems because psychotropic drugs exist. Cooperstock also questions whether the number and variety of such drugs would have proliferated were it not for the medicalizing of life problems.[13]

Defining problems of living as medical problems implies that women are psychologically incapable of coping with the stresses of life. This myth arises out of the patriarchal assumption of the medical profession that women possess inherently deficient psyches. To doctors who subscribe to this myth, it seems logical to prescribe something to help them cope. This approach leaves untouched environmental and cultural sources of women's distress and ignores the fact that the symptom may be a healthy reaction to an unhealthy situation. Sometimes, assuming that the problem is "in the woman's head," even patently physical problems which might be alleviated are bypassed. Doctors who do this may then patronizingly prescribe a psychotropic drug to pacify a patient regarded as a nuisance.[14]

In her discussion of the medical model, Anne Wilson Schaef indicts both the medical and mental health systems. Both are inherent parts of the Addictive System. Both are oriented toward control of the so-called patient. They control symptoms rather than engage in a healing process. They perpetuate the problem by fostering codependency and programming people to fit into the Addictive Society.[15]

WOMEN AND THE PHARMACEUTICAL INDUSTRY

In *Mystification and Drug Abuse*, Henry Lennard and colleagues documented highly prejudicial attitudes in the pharmaceutical industry. These authors cite several advertisements offering Valium, Librium, Vistaril, and Tofranil as treatment for conflict experienced when a young woman first goes to college, for childhood anxieties such as school and dental visits, and for parental anxiety over a runaway teenager. The advertisement suggests that normal reactions to these situations are pathological and require medical treatment. The authors conclude that when physicians prescribe drugs for life problems, they reinforce a model for a legitimate way of dealing with personal and interpersonal problems.[16] The makers of OTC drugs have great latitude in advertising because the FDA has limited control in this area. Silverman and Lee point out that the public tends to believe that OTCs are safe on the supposition that "if it wasn't safe, they would not sell it to you without a prescription."[17] However, no OTC with a biological effect can be considered entirely safe.[18] In general, advertising of OTC drugs as well as their wide use and availability promotes the habit of reaching for a pill for every discomfort.

Not only does the pharmaceutical industry collude with the medical patriarchal mythology, it also woos the medical practitioner with economic, scientific, educational, and professional bait. Lennard and colleagues describe the relationship between the drug industry and the medical profession as symbiotic. They state that the industry depends on doctors to sell their products, and to introduce and monitor new drugs through the authority of their medical status and through their exclusive use of prescriptions. In return, it provides for doctors a flow of information about its products, gives free samples, produces journals that intersperse medical information with drug propaganda, and finances medical education. Since Lennard and colleagues made this observation in 1971, little has changed in this collusive situation. The silicone implant debacle is witness to the continued exploitation of women by pharmaceutical companies.

Women are not the only victims of the Addictive Society. There are also males in the Reactive Female System. They are mainly persons of color, the poor, the handicapped, and the disadvantaged. These men are not likely to consult a physician to get help. They are more likely to abuse alcohol and/or street drugs in order to cope. Males who identify with and profit from the White Male System also suffer from stress. The competition, overwork, and anxiety that attend a life devoted to ascending the corporate ladder and outwitting competitors takes a severe toll. Some somatize stress and become victims of heart disease or cancer. Even though researchers have not given attention to the question of prescription drug abuse among middle- and upper-class males, it is quite possible that it does exist. For many men, the benefits of belonging to the Male White System are outweighed by the liabilities. However, persons addicted to power and privilege, like those suffering from substance addiction, are prone to deny consequence.

The destructive influence of the Addictive Society is not, of course, confined to adults; young persons, both male and female, are infected by its disvalues. It claims the right to set standards, and, for women, the standard of physical acceptability is one few teen girls can reach. That standard is based on what will attract the teenage boy or the young man. Early in life, the girl-child is taught to groom and behave to please others. Her sense of value is dictated by representatives of the Addictive Society. In *Fat Is a Feminist Issue*, Susan Orbach says, "Success, beauty, wealth, love, sexuality, and happiness are promoted as attached to and depending on slimness. . . . Selling body insecurity to women . . . is a vicious phenomenon."[19] The same society that sells slimness to young girls sells the bulging muscle to boys and young men. It is not a case of having healthy, well-developed muscles, but rather having a physique that exemplifies strength and power, and having it at all costs—even at the cost of one's health. With only professional athletes presented as role models, it is not surprising that many boys and young men, for whom the possibility of actually becoming a professional athlete is extremely remote, seek what seems to be within their grasp—the appearance of athletic prowess. A predominating characteristic of addiction is the worship of the quick fix. Diet pills and steroids are the ultimate quick fix prescription.

GROWING UP AND GROWING OLD

The Addictive Society is a toxic environment in which to meet the developmental crisis of youth. According to Eric Erikson, the predominate developmental task of adolescence is consolidating identity.[20] Identity means a sense of a cohesive "I" who is related to but different from others. Achieving identity is a psychosocial task that is rendered more complex and precarious than it was a hundred years ago. Part of achieving identity is making a commitment to a life work or vocation. In the White Male System, although the variety of careers is almost limitless, access to many of these is severely limited, especially for minority youth of both genders and, in spite of some progress in this regard, for many young women.

Another aspect of identity formation is the evolution of a personalized ideology. The values of the Addictive Society, however, do not appeal to many youth, specifically to those who look for altruism and to those who find themselves relegated to the peripheries of the dominant culture because of gender, race, or sexual orientation. The gap between the values some adults and institutions, such as governments and churches, profess and what they practice is often alienating to youth and more conducive of cynicism than emulation. Alienated, youth tend to form or attach themselves to subgroups where belonging is paramount. The price of belonging is often the adoption of destructive values and behaviors. Growing up in contemporary society is fraught with hazards and stress from which some find relief in the abuse of legal drugs.

Another phenomenon of the Addictive Society is that, whereas it is becoming increasingly an aging population, it is still a youth-oriented culture. According to the U.S. census, the elderly population increase during the 1979-1989 decade was five times that of younger populations.[21] Still, no longer productive and no longer powerful, the majority of the elderly in this culture are no longer valued. Most older adults were reared to believe in the work ethic, and retirement is viewed as a loss rather than an opportunity. Lacking an environment in which they can experience self-worth, they are often isolated and lonely. Yet they have grown up and grown old in the Addictive Society, have internalized its values, and are ill-prepared to face the powerlessness of old age with optimism and hope. They have participated in the Addictive Society all their lives and they may have been active addicts of one kind or another. Given all these conditions, it is not surprising that they are candidates for medication abuse or victims of so-called caregivers whose main aim is to render them passive and easily controlled. A passage in *Older Adult Substance Abuse* describes poignantly the lot of may elderly persons:

> . . . life-long coping mechanisms such as dependency on friends, getting away, receiving professional help or outside help may no longer be viable or affordable options. Developing new coping mechanisms and constructively adapting to change become necessary. When there isn't the desire to live, an overdose is one option. The mental health problems of older adults are serious and they should be addressed. Too often, drug therapy is the sole and inadequate response to the mental health problems of the aged.[22]

Like youth, older adults are negotiating a crucial developmental stage. They are making the transition from generativity to integrity. The life span has increased considerably over the past century with the result that many people enjoy (or endure) twenty years between retirement and death. Ideally, according to Erikson's schema, this is a time to consolidate one's gains, accept one's losses and inadequacies, and mature into the wisdom of old age.[23] In traditional cultures, the elderly were honored as bearers of the collective memory and repositories of the wisdom of the group. Today, they are often considered an anachronism and a burden and are ignored or neglected by their families. Loneliness and isolation as well as the absence of a meaningful place in society often generate grief and depression, from which pre-scribed drugs are a legal palliative.

The need to transcend the values and life philosophy of the Addictive Society is probably never more urgent than in old age. As one by one peers die and the elder is also faced with imminent death, the radical limitations of human power must be acknow-ledged. The person who has lived according to the precepts of the White Male System is called to evaluate her or his life in terms of ultimates. The possibility of escaping that call into workaholism or any of the other dependencies available to younger persons is no longer viable. It is extremely difficult to choose integrity now if one has, throughout life, opted for the profitable and the expe-dient. For the aging member of the Addictive Society, the moment of the ultimate "bottoming out" has arrived. The choice is integrity or despair, and often the elderly are left to face that choice alone.

HEALTH CARE IN THE ADDICTIVE SOCIETY

A salient mark of the Addictive Society is the gap between rich and poor. This gap is particularly apparent in the amount and quality of health care available to persons on opposite ends of this spectrum. Currently, even some middle-class individuals and families who are employed lack medical coverage. What health care is available to them, to the unemployed, and the poor is sparse indeed. The lack of adequate medical provision for per-sons suffering from chronic psychiatric disorders has led to seri-ous abuse of prescription and OTC drugs. There are many who receive treatment for serious disorders in outpatient clinics or from therapists willing to accept medicare. Some of these persons, for example, victims of early childhood sexual abuse, are in extreme emotional pain and should be hospitalized while receiving therapy. However, their medical insurance (if they have any) or medicare does not cover long-term psychiatric hospitalization. As a result these people, especially those who live alone, are liable to overdose or abuse prescription drugs simply in an effort to ease unbearable psychic pain. This situation causes much stress to their therapists, to their friends, and to their families.

FAMILY IN THE ADDICTIVE SOCIETY

Robert Beavers has given us a useful schema for assessing the health of families.[24] In it he classifies families from optimal to severely dysfunctional. Actual families do not necessarily fit neatly into categories; however, characteristics that delineate families in his topology are sufficiently recognizable as to make this schema helpful when applied with flexibility. I consider Beavers' description of the midrange family representative of many families in Western culture.

Midrange families are in the middle of a continuum between optimal and severely dysfunctional. Their members manage to survive, but they experience considerable pain and difficulty in functioning. Instead of seeking intimacy, these families seek control. In order to maintain control, they rule their members with inflexible norms. The family is presided over by a harsh monitor: a parent, grandparent, perfectionistic religion, or perception of God, for instance. Fear leads members to hide and feel guilty over feelings and behavior that would not meet the monitor's approval. Members tend to be overcontrolled and to respond by excessive submission or rebellion. Children feel that they must suppress qualities which do not fit family stereotypes and are often inhibited in developing individuality.

Parents in the midrange family are unequal in overt power; one dominates and the other defers. However, the less dominant one will seek power in indirect and subversive ways. Power struggles abound and are expressed in either open, angry exchanges or are masked by depression and manipulation. There is little warmth and much blaming in the family. Midrange family values do not admit ambivalence. Ambivalence toward family members is seen as evil, with the result that one side of the ambivalence is suppressed. Members often seem to be just "too nice." Children grow up psychically within a normal range but are limited. Unless they react in rebellion, they tend to conform unquestioningly to society's rules.

Midrange families come in two forms: the centripetal and the centrifugal. Centripetal families have tight boundaries. Parents are usually competent yet overly strict. One parent, usually the father, dominates. Such families may look very united from the outside, may even be considered models by others. However, their cohesion is artificial and vulnerable. They tend to suddenly show their weakness in crisis. Centrifugal families, on the other hand appear chaotic. Both parents feel and act inadequate. They blame one another for family failures. Though the mother may be the authority figure (when for instance, the father is alcoholic), the family believes in the patriarchal model. Parents in these families are seldom at home and the children are on the streets at an early age. Children run away. Parents separate; there is brawling and verbal abuse. Whereas the centripetal family is liable to produce law-abiding neurotics, the centrifugal one will produce at least some delinquents.[25]

It is not surprising that the family milieu should be a microcosm of the larger social context. The radical disorder that permeates the Addictive System has invaded every aspect of that society. The midrange family reflects the two sides of the Addictive Society: the Male White System and the Reactive Female System. The centripetal version contains a combination of both systems: the location of overt power in one parent and the reactivity in the other, the lack of intimacy and the pervasiveness of control, the demand that children conform to stereotypes (as indeed, the parents do also). The centrifugal version seems to reflect the Reactive Female System, exhibiting powerlessness and ineffectiveness. It should be noted that although the centripetal style family may look orderly and cohesive, these characteristics may mask internal disorder. Incest and abuse may take place in either style of family. It seems to me, however, that the centripetal, with its legalism and penchant for looking good, is likely to harbor legal drug abuse, while the centrifugal is liable to produce alcoholics and street-drug abusers.

Research on the families of women drug abusers shows patterns that correspond to the styles of families described above. Cuskey and Wathey note the following characteristics in the families of origin of female addicts:

- Poverty that led to family disruption, discord, and inadequate child rearing practices;
- Family disorganization caused by death, separation, or divorce;
- Parental alcoholism and, to a lesser extent, drug abuse; high instance of mental disturbance; and to a lesser extent, criminality;
- Rejecting home environment—mothers either overindulgent or cold and authoritarian, father indulgent and seductive;
- Inappropriate familial socialization resulting in inadequate sexual identity. (Studies indicated that one-fourth of female addicts had experienced incestuous sexual relationships.)[26]

Josette Mondanaro found three interacting elements involved in the etiology of female addiction: strict sex-role socialization, emotional neglect as an infant, and untimely and unrealistic performance expectation by parents. Mandanaro sees criticism for failure to meet high parental demands as a basis for the personal sense of inadequacy she found in female addicts.[27] A high parental demand for daughters is for them to be overresponsible for the well-being of the family, as their mothers are. Persons tend to marry into family systems that resemble their families of origin. Women from dysfunctional families of origin often find themselves in family situations mirroring the one into which they were born or adopted. They assume the burden of holding the family together by maintaining the stability of the system even if that stability is frozen at a dysfunctional level. They try to fulfil the stereotypical female role of providing nurturance even though they themselves may have been starved of nurturance in their family of origin. Claudia Bepko in "Disorders of Power: Women and Addiction in the Family," says that when a woman is addicted, her addiction is often a release from overresponsible thinking, feeling, and behavior, arising from her own internal overresponsibility in the family system. Women tend to view themselves as responsible even for abuse suffered at the hands of a spouse.[28]

This explanation of the etiology of the woman's addiction within the family system mirrors the imbalance of power and responsibility within the Addictive Society. The one with the least power is held most responsible and assumes the responsibility imposed on her. Her reactivity reinforces the overweening assumption of power without responsibility on the part of her spouse. Abuse of legal drugs by women is their attempt to maintain in the family their overresponsible position without corresponding power, as womankind does in the larger social milieu. The abuse of legal drugs is one of many symptoms that result from the Addictive System. Whether one becomes a workaholic, an overeater, a street drug abuser, a sexaholic, or a legal drug abuser may be affected by such idiosyncratic elements as one's physical makeup, familial or personal values, but the pervasive underlying source of these and other addictions is to be found in the sociocultural milieu. Given the discovery that a legal chemical can alleviate the pain and anxiety of life in that society, it is only a few short steps to using that chemical, then abusing it, and finally, becoming addicted to it. The outcome is not only a diminution of physical and psychological health but also increasing spiritual impoverishment. The dynamics and implications of that spiritual impoverishment will be the subject of the next chapter.

Chapter 4

Spiritual Roots of Addiction

All of us, whether or not we suffer from addiction, have one thing in common: we must live with the fact of limitation. To be human is to experience oneself as finite, yet to have longings for the infinite. The tension this condition of our existence generates has the potential for pain and joy, for achievement and for failure. We experience the hope of birth and the despair of death, the sense of power in creative accomplishments and the sense of futility when, in spite of all our achievements, we cannot eliminate suffering from the face of the earth. Philosophers and some psychologists call the tension generated by our fundamental nature "existential anxiety."

EXISTENTIAL ANXIETY

Existential anxiety is sometimes felt as a pervasive guilt arising from the fact that human achievement always falls short of potential. The longing for the infinite makes us aware that there is always more and more that might be accomplished; in the light of infinite possibilities, one can never be good enough. Theologian Karl Rahner describes the human condition in the light of ultimate yearning as:

> . . . infinite longing, radical options, discontent which cannot find rest, anguish at the insufficiency of material things, protest against death, the experience of being the object of love whose absoluteness and whose silence our mortality

cannot bear, the experience of fundamental guilt, with hope, nevertheless, remaining.[1]

For this existential guilt there is no remedy. One can only accept the fact of limitation never knowing whether or not one could or should have attained more. If the ambiguity of limitation vis-à-vis possibility is not accepted, one can become a victim of one's own or others' unrealistic expectations.

No doubt some persons experience existential anxiety more keenly than others. Genetic composition and chemical factors as well as early childhood deprivation or abuse may have rendered some more vulnerable to pain and less capable of dealing creatively with it. For such persons there is a further layer of suffering that arises from unique personal or familial factors. Individuals need to find a way to respond to existential anxiety. However, there is also a sociocultural need to create systems that provide contexts in which people may cooperate in an effort to understand and live the human situation for the benefit of all. Sociocultural endeavors to overcome human limitation have led to great technological advances to benefit humankind. Nevertheless, in many contemporary societies, the systems devised to deal with finitude often create additional and unnecessary suffering.

Inauthentic Ways to Overcome Existential Anxiety

Three inauthentic ways of seeking to overcome existential anxiety are through the acquisition of power, the experience of pleasure, and the accumulation of possessions. Power over nature and over other humans is sought in order to compensate for the radical limitations of power which inhere in being human. Pleasure helps to mask the pain that accompanies the inevitable loss of all that is held dear, even life itself. Possessions quench temporarily the human thirst for the limitless. Individuals and society itself seek to circumvent the existential human situation by one or all of these classical ways. In this sense, addictions can be understood as use of power, pleasure, and/or possessions in an attempt to deal with existential anxiety.

Existential Anxiety and the Addictive Society

Anne Wilson Schaef's analysis of the Addictive Society (discussed in the previous chapter) is an apt description of the typical societal response to existential anxiety. Western society predominantly espouses the power solution. Of course, wherever the acquisition of power arises from the need to control life and, ultimately, to control anxiety, there will always be the need for persons and things over which power can be exercised. In the Addictive Society these are nature, women, and children. This situation creates two classes of people: those who are addicted to power and those who, being powerless, become addicted to whatever gives pleasure or relieves pain because they must deal with the suffering arising from both the proximate pain of oppression and the ultimate pain of existential anxiety.

It seems to me that persons who abuse or are addicted to prescribed and over-the-counter drugs are motivated by the need to alleviate pain, increase pleasure, or gain or maintain a modicum of power. Women, girls, the elderly, and minorities are on the powerless end of the pole; men and boys, on the power end. Women whom I have known to be addicted to tranquilizers or analgesics have utilized these drugs in order to cope with an oppressive or abusive marriage relationship in which they felt trapped; to deal with the difficulties of being either actually or virtually a single parent; to subdue grief in a milieu in which they were not permitted (or could not permit themselves) to grieve; and/or to repress justified anger in a culture that does not permit women to be angry. In some cases all of these conditions existed.

Girls and young women who develop eating disorders that involve the abuse of diet pills begin that destructive course because they can no longer bear the pain of perceiving themselves as "fat and ugly" in a world where to be acceptable means measuring up to an impossible and arbitrary standard of beauty. Some have been sexually abused and are unconsciously trying to look asexual in order to avoid undesired attention, or have come to experience their bodies as bad because of the abuse.

Abuse of licit drugs among boys and men also has sociocultural roots. Literature on the topic of dependency on over-the-counter and prescribed drugs indicates that the number of males involved is much smaller than that of females. Some males whom I have encountered who have had this problem perceived themselves as powerless and weak and felt stigmatized because they were weak in a world which demanded that males be strong and powerful. A few were homosexual and were ashamed of their sexual orientation, and some had been victims of childhood sexual abuse. Some men and boys see steroids as an answer to the need to at least look powerful by acquiring and maintaining an excessively muscular physique. The assertion that legal drug abuse is an attempt to deal with both existential anxiety and difficulties arising from social systems created to overcome or evade that same anxiety does not account, however, for the fact that some persons become abusers of over-the-counter and prescription drugs and some do not. It would seem that there are some further conditions operant. The legal drug abuser is usually a person who conforms to the system. This type of abuse is more acceptable than the abuse of illegal drugs. It fits the cultural requirement of conformity to societal norms. Moreover, the choice of a drug may have been related to the coincidental use of the drug and its alleviation of psychic pain or the drugs potential to give its user the desired physique.

Persons recovering from drug addiction as well as those involved in counseling drug addicts have long been aware of the demonic power the addiction has over its victim. When we understand that the drug is used as a remedy for the primary and secondary pain and limitations of the human condition, it is understandable that it would have such power. Traditionally, religion has claimed to be the system that provides the means to live out the human condition with its attendant anxiety in such a way as to find meaning in its sufferings and to celebrate its joys. Whatever replaces religion partakes of its archetypal power in the psyche of the person. Shirley, a woman recovering from ten years of addiction to a tranquilizer, described the radical hold her addiction had on her in this way, "I could not live with it; I could not live without it. I would have sold my soul to get it, yet I knew it was destroying me. It had become a devouring god."

RELIGION AND SPIRITUALITY

Effective recovery programs have recognized the spiritual roots of addiction and have a built-in spiritual dimension. Alcoholics Anonymous and other twelve-step programs believe that the acknowledgment of and a relationship to a Higher Power is fundamental to lasting recovery. However, they are quick to deny that they are religious programs; instead, they prefer to refer to themselves as spiritual programs. Though these terms are sometimes used interchangeably, it is important to recognize a differ ence between them.

Religion is a system of beliefs, rituals, and codes of behavior into which one was born or which one may have joined. It originates outside the person. Spirituality, on the other hand, is rooted in the personal and collective experience of the Sacred. It has a variety of practices that aim to nurture the relationship with the Sacred. Both religion and spirituality have external structures. However, the validating norms for religion are past and present authorities, whereas the validating norms for spiritualities are the individual and collective experience of the Sacred, discerned in community with other seekers of the Ultimate, and in continuity with the spiritual wisdom of the past.

Ideally, religion and spirituality are interrelated, each drawing on the insights and structures of the other, each acting as a corrective for the other. However, far from the ideal, it has been more customary for each to suspect and distrust the other. Spiritualities have sometimes resisted the control religions have sought to exercise over them. At times, religions have looked on spirituality as idiosyncratic and doctrinally irresponsible. Churches have tended to promote religion rather than spirituality, with the result that the spirituality of the average church member has remained largely in remission. Without dialogue with spirituality, religions and their theologies have tended to become increasingly more abstract and cerebral. They have sought to hold coercive power over their members, promoting obedience to the religious authority over the personal and collective discernment of the action of the Spirit in their lives. Moreover, Western religious systems have been closely patterned after the patriarchal model of the cultures in which they were founded. Whereas God is believed to be spirit and therefore without gender, those in power insist on naming God by masculine names: Father, Lord, King. Because they associate power with the nature of God and associate God with the male gender, they tend to support and validate the culture's proclivity for ascribing characteristics associated with power to males and ascribing characteristics associated with weakness to females. Their normative theologies have been formulated by males from a male perspective, and although they may proclaim gender equality, they exhibit inequality of power and position in ways similar to those found in secular cultures. They exhibit most of the characteristics Anne Wilson Schaef delineates as typical of the White Male System. In fact, she includes churches explicitly in that system.[2]

The Reactive Female System

According to Schaef, women in the White Male System (to which the majority of religions belong) must alter the way in which they view the world in order to survive. They must adopt the language, values, and beliefs of the dominant system. To gain acceptance, they must deny their own reality and surrender personal power. They are trapped in an externally defined system that tells them what they should think, feel, and do. This is the Reactive Female System that is related symbiotically to and supports the White Male System and its myths.[3] I would add here that there are probably a considerable number of men who, because of their marginalized position in the culture, belong to the Reactive Female System as it is described above.

RELIGION AND RECOVERY FROM ADDICTION

It is not surprising that many persons in recovery from addiction wake up to the realization that they have been oppressed and damaged by the very religions that professed to be their saviors. This situation creates a crisis for the addicted persons; they find that religion, their primary savior, and the drug, their substitute religion, have both failed them. Yet, they are powerless over their addiction. They need to draw on a power greater than their finite selves. This movement—from dependence on a religious system or on a drug to dependence on an Absolute, experienced not merely outside of themselves, but also within them—when it takes place, is a leap of faith and hope. It is a conversion. There is, moreover, a subtle but important distinction between dependence on a religion and reliance on an Absolute Power experienced within as well as outside of oneself. The former is liable to be simply another addiction; the latter is likely to be the foundation for empowerment.

WOMEN AND RELIGION

In her novelette, *The Awakening,* Kate Chopin describes the heroine, Edna Pontillier, as follows:

> Mrs. Pontillier was beginning to realize her position in the universe as a human being and to recognize her relationship

as an individual to the world within and about her. This may seem like a ponderous weight of wisdom to descend on the soul of a young woman of twenty-eight.[4]

Edna is a woman who has glimpsed in childhood, through a natural, mystical experience, the open possibilities of her being. She recalls memories ". . . of a summer day in Kentucky, of a meadow that seems as big as the ocean to the very little girl walking through grass which was higher than her waist. She threw out her arms as if swimming as she walked, beating the tall grass as one strikes water." Carol Christ calls this awakening a spiritual conversion. "It concerns Edna's recognition of the nature and potential of her soul." Edna begins to become aware of the negative qualities of her marriage, of the way she had relinquished her selfhood in subservience to her husband.[5]

After her husband had awakened her to care for the children who were asleep and did not need her attention, she went out to the porch to cry. "An indescribable oppression which seemed to generate in some unfamiliar part of her consciousness filled her whole being with a vague anguish." Chopin tells us that "even as a small child, (Edna) had lived her own small life all within herself. At a very early period she had apprehended instinctively that outward existence which conforms, the inward life which questions."[6] This description of Edna Pontillier is, I believe, a description of Everywoman. In the outer world are the societal and religious norms which state who she is supposed to be, and within is the still small voice of her spirit telling her who she is and who she can become.

Ideally, the truth of woman's inner being should be complemented and validated by the truths of religion, but unfortunately, this rarely happens. Theologies of whatever domination are the descendants of forefathers who accepted unquestioningly and incorporated into their systems the contradictory beliefs that women are, by nature, on the one hand, weak, seductive, powerful, and evil, and on the other hand, pure, innocent, celestial, and all loving. They are to be feared, controlled, even exterminated, and also revered, protected, and even worshipped. Some religions legitimize the division of women into two kinds: the whore/witch and the virgin/saint, providing motivation and excuse for the oppression of "bad" women and the protection and idolizing of "good" women. Absorbing the distortions and untruths that have been foisted on her by patriarchal religions, woman has lost contact with her own center. However, there is a sense in which she cannot entirely suppress the truth of herself. Within herself each woman knows that she is neither of these stereotypes, that she must weave from the threads of the wisdom of her foremothers, the insights of her enlightened sisters and brothers, and the guidance of the Spirit within her, the unique creation she can become. Fidelity to this life work, however, brings suffering, in some instances so daunting that the work is abandoned or, in some cases, never begun.

The Inner and Outer World

Many women feel torn between the inner world of their own perceptions of reality and the outer world, socially constructed and interpreted by men. This problem has several dimensions. First, and perhaps most fundamental, woman's very consciousness has been radically affected by having, for generations, internalized a male perception of herself and the world. Often it is difficult for a woman to distinguish her own truth from a culturally fabricated version of who she is and who she ought to be. This tendency to try to live out of myths about herself alienates woman from herself and from others, especially from women who have divested themselves of the same myths.

Second, living out of her own truth brings woman into conflict with others. Formed by nature and nurture toward valuing relationships, and forced to choose between personal integrity and a harmonious relationship with persons who are important to them, women must pay a high price for their integrity. Lacking a theology that validates her true self, subjected to criticism and opposition from those who carry power and authority in her church, some women become discouraged or intimidated and settle for an uneasy half-life which permits them to survive but denies them the fullness of life promised by their various religions.

Religions, in so far as they reflect and legitimize sociocultural mores and arrangements, provide a milieu in which even women's sinfulness is seen as virtue and her healthy aspirations seen as sin. Valerie Saiving Goldstein, one of the first to point to this phenomenon, states that contemporary theology defines sin in terms of "pride, will-to-power, exploitation, self-assertiveness" and conceives of redemption as restoring to humans what they "fundamentally lack: sacrificial love, the I-Thou relationship, the primacy of the personal, peace."[7] However, this definition of sin is based on a perception of the fundamental elements of male sin. Goldstein goes on to say that the temptations of women are not the same as those of men. While pride and will-to-power, especially power over women, designates appropriately the fundamental male sin, woman's original sin is quite the opposite. It lies, rather, in her will to subordination, her lack of the courage to become, to name and resist the forces that oppress her.[8]

Few today can be unaware of the concrete shape of human sinfulness that results from male will-to-power and female will-to-please. Frequently we hear of women who remain in abusive situations either because they blame themselves, or believe (sincerely) that if they leave and take legal action, they risk being blamed for their own abuse. In a less dramatic way, women will accept verbal and behavioral put-downs without protest, for fear of offending members of the dominant group. Again, this fear of offending is sometimes proven justified when women who complain of sexual harassment are demoted or deprived of their jobs.

Related to passivity in the face of abuse is the tendency to respond in indirect ways. Women, more than men, feel guilty about feeling or expressing anger. (This guilt is an outcome of religious and cultural norms of female goodness.) Hence they tend to manifest anger in disguised ways: by withdrawing and becoming depressed, becoming physically ill, becoming self-abusive, or even attempting suicide. Women whom I have known to be dependent on prescribed or over-the-counter drugs have frequently been enduring unfair, oppressive, and even abusive situations. Their self-destructive abuse of these drugs may well have been their indirect reactions to or ways of enduring conditions which should have provoked anger and subsequent action taken on their own behalf.

Males are also ill-served by religious systems which espouse patriarchy. When the weight of religion is given to the myth of innate male superiority and the legitimizing of male power, masculine alienation from the so-called weaker characteristics of humanness—vulnerability, compassion, tenderness—is aggravated. Maintaining positions of power and exercising undue control whether in the home, in the world of work, or of nature, demand a price, often the physical and emotional health of many men. While such religions would condemn the abuse (and sometimes even the use) of alcohol, ordinarily, they have nothing to say about the abuse of prescription and OTC drugs. These legal drugs can easily become a recourse for men suffering from the pain which attends their lives.

RELIGIOUS SYSTEMS AS PART OF THE ADDICTIVE SOCIETY

What is most distressing about many religious systems is that whereas they are the main source of meaning and power for humans in living out the paradoxes of their humanity, they themselves are a part of the Addictive Society. Religious systems and mores are meant to help humankind to respond creatively to the fundamental human condition of being finite with infinite aspirations. However, instead of providing a context in which to live out this existential tension, religions often impose a superstructure which adds to that tension and anxiety. It is understandable that some persons will become addicted to a substance that promises to alleviate the pain of both levels of tension. However, as addicted persons discover, that promise is inevitably betrayed. The addiction itself creates another level of anxiety and pain.

Spirituality, on the other hand, is a way of discovering one's fundamental relationship to the sacred ground of all reality. It is in this relationship to the Sacred (the Holy, God, Ultimate Wisdom, or whatever other name is ascribed to this source of all life) that humans find a way to embrace and live the condition of being mortal and limited, yet longing for the immortal and the infinite. Embarking on the spiritual journey involves a conversion. It means letting go of the hope of being rescued from one's addiction, from the religious and cultural conditions in which one is embedded, and from the fundamental conditions of being human. This conversion, whether it happens suddenly or is a gradual series of steps, involves a disciplined commitment to a way of life that will involve struggle and pain and will require the support of other committed pilgrims. This way of life involves a growing sense of one's connectedness with the universe, of being at home in the world of nature. For this reason, the practice of meditation is an integral part of a healthy life as well as an important component of recovery.

As discussed in this chapter, addiction has roots at two levels. It is fundamentally a destructive way of responding to the tension and pain that arise from being human. It is also a way of coping with the suffering that arises from society's efforts to escape the limits of the human condition. An effective pastoral response must address the roots of addiction at both levels.

Chapter 5

Pastoral Response

Pastoral caregivers are in a paradoxical position vis-à-vis the problem of the abuse of prescription and over-the-counter drugs. On the one hand, they are often in a position to detect abuse, and they may also be in positions of trust and influence from which they might make successful interventions. However, as representatives of religious institutions, they may be unknowingly embedded in the Addictive Society and, therefore, part of the problem.

The first hazard attached to being part of the problem is a tendency to deny that a problem exists. The second is that even when a problem is recognized at the symptomatic level, there may be a blindness to its multiple roots. Pastoral ministers who decide to reach out to the drug-dependent person are embarking on a journey that may force them to examine critically their assumptions about church or synagogue, religious systems, and their social constructions of reality.

The first step in being helpful to persons caught in the web of addiction to legal drugs is to develop an awareness that the problem is widespread and that during the course of a day one may meet several people afflicted with this disorder. The pastor in a parish should be alert to the possibility that many women and even some men in her/his congregation may be abusing prescription or over-the-counter drugs. The lay pastoral caregiver will meet many people in the course of ministry who are using prescribed drugs to cope with the very life situations which are the context of ministry: grief, family problems, marital prob-

lems, financial difficulties, and so forth. A number of girls in the
youth group are likely to be abusing diet pills; a number of boys
to be pumping themselves up with steroids. Children in private
schools run by churches and religious communities are abusing
various kinds of pills. Co-ministers may be popping tranquilizers, courting burnout and collapse, even as they seek to tend the
needs of others. Nursing home visitors and ministers to elderly
shut-ins are probably talking frequently to overmedicated and
oversedated elders. Pastoral counselors in centers or in private
practice possibly have many clients who are suffering from
unrecognized medication addiction. Spiritual directors may be
futilely discoursing on methods of prayer with persons whose
spiritual and psychological maladies may be well hidden behind
a tranquilized haze.

A pastoral response to this problem requires a two-tiered
approach. The first step involves intervention and, where possible, help to set the individual abuser on the path toward recovery. The second step calls for the recognition that drug abuse is a
symptom that something is amiss in the social system and for a
thorough examination of that system and intervention aimed at
change. I will illustrate the need for this two-pronged approach
by way of a parable.

A certain man walking on the bank of a river that flows
through an industrial area of the state noticed several fish lying
dead on the bank and several others gasping for breath in the
water. The man hurried off, and purchased a net and a large tank.
He returned to the river, captured the fish, and placed them in a
tank of fresh water, where for several weeks he tended them with
food and medicine. The fish recovered and became healthy.
When they were quite well he returned them to the river, where, a
couple of weeks later, they died. A woman was also walking
along the same river and she too noticed the dead and dying fish.
She hurried off to the environmental protection agency and
demanded that something be done about the pollution of the

river. She mobilized public opinion and formed an influential group who were able to bring about the prosecution of the polluting industries. Within a year, the pollutants had been entirely removed from the river, but by that time most of the fish had died. Obviously the problem of the dying fish needed a both/and, rather than an either/or response. An effective pastoral program for drug abuse also involves features of both types of response.

CARING FOR THE INDIVIDUAL

Opportunities for intervention at the individual level occur in the ordinary course of ministry, pastoral care, or pastoral counseling. A classroom teacher in a school or in a Sunday school program or a youth minister may notice that a teen girl has had a drastic weight loss in recent months. This adult may express concern to the girl involved and inquire about how she is doing. If a level of trust has already been established in the ministerial context, the teen may speak about problems, including her concern about weight. A typical conversation might run as follows:

Minister: How have things been going for you, Allison?

Allison: Ok, I guess. I'm going to try out for the cheerleading squad again this year. Last year I did not make it, but I think I have a really good chance this time.

Minister: That takes courage. I remember how disappointed you were last year when you weren't chosen. What do you think of your chances this time?

Allison: Oh, I think I have a real good chance this year. See, I have lost a lot of the flab and I've worked real hard on the routines.

Minister: Yes, I have noticed that you have gotten very thin; you looked quite good as you were, though.

Do you think weight featured in last year's choices?

Allison: [sounding a little bitter] Oh, sure it did. It always does. The kids with the great "bods" are always the ones who get chosen.

Minister: [repressing the desire to defend the school and protest that Allison is mistaken] Feeling that you had the talent and that you were unfairly handicapped must have been very hurtful for you.

Allison: It sure was, but this time I'm all set to win.

Minister: Was losing that weight hard?

Allison: [looking embarrassed] Yeah, at first. . . . You're not going to like this . . . [with a rush of confidence] I got these pills and they really helped. Now I don't feel like eating so much.

Minister: [trying to sound casual] Pills?

Allison: Don't get mad at me! I got them from a friend. They're not illegal or anything. Her Mom got them from a doctor.

Minister: Allison, I'm not mad at you, but I am a bit concerned that you are using medication prescribed for someone else. You know that can be dangerous.

Allison: You don't have to worry. They're not addictive or anything. Anyhow, I'm not taking them any more . . . don't need to. I can just regulate what I eat much better now. [briskly] Well, I've got to go to practice.

Minister: Good luck with the tryouts. Let me know how you get on.

This kind of conversation presupposes that a level of trust has already been established between the teacher or youth minister and the young person. This is the advantage of having a context in which to build a relationship of care and trust prior to the emergence of a problem. The above conversation opens the possibility of discovering if medication abuse is taking place and of confronting the person with its dangers and the need for help. There is a need for patience if the intervention is to be successful. The need to supply a remedy precipitously may harden the resistance and undermine trust rather than build a foundation for treatment and recovery. This conversation indicates that this young girl may still be using pills (even though she is denying it) and that she may already be somewhat anoretic. There will be a need for many caring and careful follow-up conversations before she is ready to admit the extent of the problem. Allison may even avoid the teacher, who will have to seek her out in an unthreatening way.

A similar scenario might take place between a teacher or a coach and an adolescent boy who is abusing steroids. Access to a college-level male or to a professional athlete would be more difficult to achieve. However, even in these cases a campus minister or a chaplain might have the opportunity to observe and suspect abuse and to broach the subject with the person concerned.

Pastoral caregivers have access to persons who may knowingly or unknowingly be abusing medication. They get to know the elderly and their families when they visit nursing homes or shut-ins in their own homes. Those who have a talent for picking up clues in casual conversation and pursuing them in a caring and unthreatening way are in a good position to make initial interventions in situations where medication is being abused. As with adolescents, having established a trust relationship with the elderly is imperative if the intervention is to be successful. The resistance of elders to direct confrontation is specifically noted in *Effective Substance Abuse Counseling with Specific Groups.*

> Most older adults, . . . withdraw from a confrontational approach and refuse to admit the problem or enter treat-

ment. Such an approach is seen by the elderly as a lack of respect and an insult to their integrity. In addition, most older adults were raised with the belief that it is not proper for others to discuss their problems. Their response is often negative when another individual insists on discussing a matter which they consider to be very private. The elderly tend to respond much more positively to an indirect inquiry about their substance abuse once the counselor has built rapport.[1]

A pastoral visitor might, in the case of an elder who is suspected of medication abuse, begin a conversation by enquiring if the medication is helping and if it is causing any side effects.

Recovery from medication abuse and/or addiction requires a team approach; no individual caregiver possesses all the skills required to see a person firmly established on that road. The person who facilitates the first step—recognition and ownership of the problem—may be a pastoral care specialist or a pastoral counselor who is seeing someone whose presenting problem may be depression, family or marital problems, or anything other than drug addiction. He or she is the one who will companion the recoverer through a long process involving medical, psychological, and spiritual help. The following is a composite description of a pastor's involvement in the recovery of a woman addicted to tranquilizers. The context here is a generic Christian church; however, the reader may image a similar scenario taking place in a church or synagogue of choice, substituting the relevant pastoral resources and practices.

Mariah approaches her pastor, Charlene, to talk about her husband's drinking.

Mariah: [looking nervous, hands shaking, approached Pastor Charlene after Sunday services] Pastor, I need to talk to you about something when you have time.

Charlene: I can see you in the church office in five minutes if you don't mind waiting. I have just a few things to finish up.

Charlene: [a little later, entering the office where Mariah is seated leafing through a magazine] I'm glad we could get together right away; you seem upset about something.

Mariah: [bursting into tears] Everything has been going wrong recently. My husband, Bill, he's been out of work for six months now, and no prospect of employment. I know its hard on him, but he's been drinking, and he yells at me and the kids. I think sometimes I cannot stand it any longer. . . . I've been having these terrible headaches. . . . [breaking off in sobs]

Charlene: [offering a box of tissues and waiting for the sobbing to subside] You are really going through an ordeal and I can see that you are in a lot of pain. Have you been getting any help with all of this?

Mariah: Well, my doctor gave me some nerve pills after little Ryan was born a year ago and then a month ago he gave me something to help me to sleep . . . with the baby and all this trouble and keeping my job going, I haven't been getting more than a few hours . . . recently nothing seems to help . . . I'm shaking all the time and sometimes I have these weird sensations. . . . I think I'm going crazy. Do you think I'm going crazy? [more sobbing]

When Mariah regains her composure, Charlene asks her if she knows the name of the little "nerve pills." She shows her a bottle of Valium; the label reads, "Valium 10 mgs. three times a day or as needed." Mariah has been taking them "as needed" and cannot remember how often. She has also been taking Seconal to help her to sleep.

Charlene: Mariah, did you know that these strange sensations you are experiencing could be the effects of the drugs you are taking?

Mariah: Oh no, my doctor told me they were quite safe so long as I followed the prescription.

Charlene: Well, Mariah, you seem to have been taking a pretty high dosage over a long period of time and Valium has been found to cause symptoms like the ones you're experiencing, especially when it is mixed with other chemicals. I know a couple of doctors who have special training and experience with problems arising from medical drugs; would you be willing to see one of them to have your medication evaluated?

Mariah: It would be a relief if these feelings turned out to be only the pills, but I wouldn't want to offend Dr. Johnson by going to someone else.

Charlene: Looking out for yourself makes you feel disloyal to Dr. Johnson?

Mariah: Yes, I guess that's how it is; though when you put it that way, it does seem foolish.

Charlene: Mariah, your well-being is more important than any doctor's feelings. Anyhow, you have a perfect right to seek another opinion. The doctors I have mentioned are Dr. Helen Hunter and Dr. Sam Rosen. If you agree to see one of them, I would be glad to give you their phone numbers.

Mariah: Well, if you think I should, I'll go ahead and do it because I am really at the end of my rope.

When Mariah is checked out by a physician, she is found to have a high level of Valium in her blood and to have become addicted to the drug. She is admitted to a drug dependency treatment center. In the course of group therapy, Mariah discloses that she has been taking more Valium than prescribed. Her therapist at the center involves all the family in the treatment, and during one of the sessions, Jim's drinking comes up. He admits that his drinking has been a long-standing problem and that previous attempts to control it have failed. Jim is admitted to the outpatient program. He agrees to take antabuse, but steadfastly refuses to attend AA, insisting that he can lick the problem with the help of antabuse. Charlene visits the unit occasionally to give Mariah support in her treatment. During one of the visits they discuss Mariah's feeling of guilt at disgracing the family by being a "drug addict." Later, when Mariah had acquired a better understanding of the history and nature of her drug abuse, she summed up her perception of guilt this way: "It's meaningless to blame myself or anyone else; I need to devote my energy to carrying out my responsibility to do all I can to recover. What happened to me could have happened to anyone in my situation."

Charlene also visits with Mariah's family. She meets Mariah's husband, Jim, and commends him for having taken steps to deal with his drinking. In the course of the conversation, she brings up the subject of AA and discovers that Jim has attended one meeting at the hospital but that he felt out of place because all the men there were professionals and Jim is a blue-collar worker. Charlene asks Jim if he would be willing to go to another meeting with a member of their church who is recovering from alcoholism, and who, like Jim, is a truck driver. Jim agrees to give AA another try.

While Charlene is in the home, Donna, the fifteen-year-old daughter comes in from school. Charlene tries to engage her in conversation but she answers sullenly and escapes as soon as she can. Her father admits that he has been particularly hard on

Donna and that he had called her a tramp because she had dated a gang member against his wishes. After two sessions, she has refused to attend the hospital program for teens. Charlene decides to ask the youth minister to contact Donna and try to befriend her.

After six weeks, Mariah is discharged from the hospital program, but she continues to attend a group called Pills Anonymous; she also attends Al-Anon. Six months later, Mariah and Jim are still working with their programs. Charlene invites them to a parent's retreat and arranges for a volunteer to sit the younger children so that Donna will be free to go on an outing with the youth group. During the course of the retreat, the subject of family conflict, hurt, and reconciliation is discussed. Mariah and Jim say that they have come a long way in understanding one another and in making amends. However, they admit that though Jim has apologized to Donna, she is still very cold and distant toward him. Jim breaks down and weeps as he talks about the remorse he feels over the harm he has done his family, especially Donna. He resolves to continue to try to make amends to her. As a result of her contact with other women during the retreat, Mariah begins to attend a women's spiritual growth group.

Charlene has continued to keep in contact with this family in order to monitor how they are doing and to encourage them in their recovery. She has tried to involve Donna in an Alateen group but without success. As a result of this experience with Mariah, Charlene realizes that there may be others in the parish who are dependent on various drugs. She asks the leaders in the parish council to organize an addiction awareness Sunday with an aim to provide information on the various forms of dependency and the help available to those afflicted or affected by them. On that Sunday, the service is centered around human weakness and healing, and a person recovering from an addiction preaches the sermon in which he speaks about his own experience of drug addiction and recovery. The congregation is invited to view a choice of short videos on various dependencies, procure literature on these topics, and talk to representatives from the local hospital and drug and alcoholism treatment centers. Care is taken to include the less known dependencies such as those which afflict the aging, dependencies on legal drugs, on diet pills, and on food. The entire program is planned and carried out by volunteers from various twelve-step programs.

A RECOVERY PROGRAM

Even though the roots of addiction are embedded in the social milieu, the problem is not first addressed at that level. Chemical addiction, once established, becomes an autonomous malady which, even if the Addictive Society were to change, would run its separate course. Moreover, there is no guarantee that the social milieu will recover from its addiction to power, pleasure, and possession. It is important that the individual seek health regardless of whether or not the culture does so. Recovery from drug dependency involves physical, psychological, spiritual, and systemic dimensions, for the individual. The following schema indicates the major issues that need to be addressed on these levels.

Detoxification

The first step in recovery is interrupting the addiction cycle. The person physically addicted to the drug is likely to be unable to withstand withdrawal when use of the drug is discontinued and may return to abusing the drug simply to alleviate these symptoms. Detoxification can take several weeks depending on the drug, the dosage, and the length of time the person has been taking it. Because withdrawal symptoms may be severe and even life-threatening, detoxification should be conducted under medical supervision and may require hospitalization. The pastoral minister's support and encouragement are imperative during this trying phase of recovery. This is a pastoral opportunity to contact the family and to encourage them to avail of a recovery program.

Medical Assessment

The drug-dependent person should have physical assessment in order to ascertain if there is an illness that may have preceded the drug abuse and also to determine if the abuse has caused any physical damage. Physical disorders, if left untreated, may precipitate the recurrence of the drug abuse. Persons who have been abusing diet pills may also be anoretic or bulimic and may be suffering from serious malnutrition requiring medical treatment. Steroids are known to cause a number of disorders; among them are liver disease, high blood pressure, tumors, and hypercalcemia, all of which require medical treatment.[2]

Psychotherapy

Withdrawal also involves emotional disturbances such as depression, anxiety, and mood swings. The recovering person will need support counseling in order to understand and deal with these disturbances. Moreover, there may be a preexisting psychic disorder such as unipolar or bipolar depression, post-traumatic stress syndrome, schizophrenia, borderline personality disorder, and so forth, which played a part in the drug misuse in the first place. Women and girls who abuse medications may have an unacknowledged history of sexual abuse. Elder abusers may be suffering from senility or undiagnosed Alzheimer's disease. Sometimes medication abuse causes conditions that mimic these disorders in elders.

Some persons, especially women, are prescribed sedatives at the time of a death of a spouse, the loss of a child, a miscarriage, or a divorce. The sedative, rather than helping, may have blocked normal grieving, and behind the medication abuse, there may be

a logjam of unresolved grief. For these individuals, grief counseling is imperative. Often, the medication abuser has used drugs
to cope with normal life problems. The adolescent may have
used them to alleviate anxiety attached to negotiating social relationships, identity issues, and sexual adjustment. The adult
woman may have used them to deal with transition points in the
family life cycle: adjustment in the early years of marriage,
increase in family membership through birth or adoption, rearing
teen children, the departure of young adults from the family,
menopause, etc. Such persons may have to learn for the first time
how to handle productively life's crises and transitions. Learning
adaptive and unlearning maladaptive coping skills are also a part
of recovery therapy.

Older adults have to deal with the losses associated with
aging: the loss of a sense of worth when they are no longer
employed, loneliness and isolation occasioned by the loss of
peers through death and of family who have moved away or been
alienated. There is also the loss of physical powers such as loss
of mobility, hearing, and sight, all of which diminish self-worth
and add to their isolation and loneliness. These problems may
have played a part in their medication abuse and are still there in
an aggravated form when they have stopped abusing. These need
to be addressed in a therapeutic situation.

Family Therapy

Frequently, the abuse of medication in one or another member
of a family is a symptom of dysfunctionality in the family system. Sometimes the dysfunctionality may be located in the family of origin of the abuser. There may have been a history of
physical abuse or alcoholism or other addictive behavior which
have left unhealed wounds. There may be dysfunctionality in the
present nuclear family that precipitated the drug abuse. Family
systems therapy can help to uncover the general dysfunctionality
being masked by the symptom and bring about systemic change

so that the family will no longer need the identified patient's symptom in order to maintain an unhealthy balance. Without systemic change, the medication abusing family member will have great difficulty continuing to recover while remaining a part of the family system.

As is the case with any other substance abuse, the behavior of the designated patient is co-dependent on the behavior of other family members. Some will have assumed the role of enabler by shielding the person from the consequence of her addiction. Others will have assumed the role of victim by accepting passively the pain occasioned by the drug abuser's behavior. These roles do not automatically fade away when recovery begins. They may be clung to and become an impediment to recovery.

Because overmedication may have made the elderly more manageable, family members may have given tacit encouragement to this form of drug abuse. Moreover, the recovery of the abuser will disturb the balance in the family system, which has occurred around the drug abuse. She may refuse to accept the subordinate position she has occupied previously. The recovery of a child or teen whose addiction has been the glue which kept the parental marriage together may destabilize the marriage. The recovering person may, for instance, begin to claim more authority and power, thereby unbalancing the one-sided distribution of power in the family system. Because recovery initiates a disturbance in family homeostasis, it is likely to be resisted by family members even as they consciously advocate it.

Counseling for drug abuse is liable to uncover serious problems within the family, such as physical and/or sexual abuse. For instance, the previous scenario above might have taken a different direction. Mariah's drug abuse might have been a way of coping with physical abuse; her daughter Donna's sullen resistance to engagement in the family therapy sessions might have been a reaction to incest the family had not acknowledged. Counselors and caregivers involved with families such as these need to be alert to hints of deeper hidden problems and shameful family secrets masked by the addictive or rebellious behavior.

Claudia Bepko recommends that in the case of women substance abusers family therapy be undertaken in three phases. In the first phase, treatment deals mainly with the "the systemic relationship between the addict and the drug of choice, as well as all the other systemic responses that maintain that relationship."[3] In the second phase, the larger family system becomes the focus of therapy as it adjusts to the abuser's recovery. In the third phase, the family itself is helped to maintain a healthy balance that will prevent abuse from recurring in the next generation. Utilizing a three phase system makes it possible for therapists to decide who shall be included in the therapy at the various stages. Bepko argues persuasively for working primarily with the woman alone in the beginning phases. This approach has been judged antifeminist because it gives the impression that the woman is to blame and seems to place all the responsibility on her by making her the "identified patient." However, Bepko defends this approach by explaining:

> Work with women may indeed put the initial burden of change on the woman, but change is in the direction of destabilizing the system, challenging the existing power imbalances and refuting society's definition of the woman as sick. Her addiction is viewed, not as a pathology, but as her attempt at health. That is, the addiction is viewed as her expression of defiance against her one-down status or at least her need to tranquilize herself into accepting the unacceptable.[4]

With due attention to the suggestion that the woman's addiction should be viewed as her attempt at health, I believe that Ms. Bepko's three-phase structure might indeed be profitably adopted by therapists.

Couple Counseling

Sometimes marital problems, including a husband's alcoholism and physical abuse, bring women to medical doctors with symptoms of anxiety, depression, headaches, menstrual disorders, or sexual dysfunctions. Without seeking the underlying problem, the doctor may prescribe tranquilizers, on which, lacking any other way of coping, the woman becomes dependent. Lasting recovery necessitates real change in the marital relationship, not an alternative way of coping with an oppressive situation. Recovery may mean that the marriage cannot or should not endure. In this case the counselor needs to be ready to initiate divorce counseling.

Assertiveness Training

Drug-dependent women (and in some cases men) do not know how to get their needs met. They are usually schooled in taking care of others while enduring oppressive conditions in the home and on the job. Years of actually being helpless to bring about change has conditioned them to believe that change is never possible. They lack the skills to stand firm, to say "No" to unreasonable demands. To counteract this programming, they need extensive training in assertiveness skills. Males who have had their needs met through aggressive behavior need training in substituting verbal assertiveness for physical aggression. Both need to learn how to be appropriately dependent, to ask for help when they need it, and to give and receive nurturance.

Vocational Training

Women recovering from medication abuse may need to enter or reenter the job market but do not know what direction to pursue. They may need help in assessing their talents and in further training for a job or a career. Older adults, especially males forced into early retirement, may need help in locating a part-time or volunteer occupation in which they can feel productive. Males, such as Mariah's husband who have been unemployed, sometimes because of their substance abuse, may need help to find employment. Some adolescents, because of inadequate education, have few skills; they need special remedial help in order to qualify for even simple jobs. They may also need help to obtain positions during times of economic recession. Having skills can help them to build self-esteem, the lack of which may have been instrumental in their abusing drugs.

Health Education

Health education should be holistic in its thrust, covering both physical and emotional issues. As a group, the elderly have the highest incidence of medical and psychiatric disorders and are prescribed a variety of drugs. Because of the physiological effects, they usually require lower dosages. They may also react unpredictably to specific drugs. However, they may fail to understand the reason certain drugs are being prescribed or their side effects. Women and the elderly are particularly liable to defer to a doctor's opinion and to abdicate their right to know what they are being prescribed and why, and to make personal choices regarding their health care. Health education should inform them about their rights and responsibilities.

Youth, who feel immortal, need education in the actual dangers of the misuse of legal drugs. There is a tendency to want to believe that if something is called medicine or is sold over the counter, it cannot do one harm. All legal drug abusers need education on how drugs function in the body, their potential for healing, and their potential for harm. Some persons who abuse pain killers do so in order to control chronic pain. They need to be informed about alternative ways of controlling pain. In these cases, referral to pain clinics may be in order.

Self-Help Group Work

Women and elders recovering from medication addiction are likely to resist group involvement. Unlike alcohol consumption, taking medical drugs is not a social activity. Women in general and female drug abusers in particular have low self-esteem. They find it easier to discuss their problems with one person than to risk rejection by revealing them to members of a group. As stated earlier, elders often feel they need to keep their problems private. However, both these groups can benefit from participating in recovery groups. Meeting others who are struggling with similar problems breaks the isolation which often afflicts the elderly and women. Interacting with persons who are more advanced in the recovery process helps to give hope and courage to beginners. Teen abusers need to connect with others who understand their struggles and who are in recovery, otherwise they are liable to return to social networks in which they are reintroduced to drug abuse.

Consciousness Raising

Persons who abuse medications, whether they are women, men, elders, or adolescents, are likely to be uncritical acceptors of socially constructed perceptions of their identity, their worth, and their role. In fact their abuse of such drugs is often related to the stress occasioned by their attempts to fit into or adjust to stereotypical perceptions of reality. For women and men, these perceptions demand that they conform to socially defined roles of self-effacing nurturer or aggressive manager and provider, respectively. Even though most people are aware of the movement in the past thirty years to challenge these stereotypes, the embedded hold they have on the identities of persons who grew up in strictly role-defined families and cultures is still but minimally influenced by changes that are more theoretical than actual. Youth of both genders are still pressured to strive for the ideally feminine and ideally masculine, images still cast in the traditional sex-role mold. This problem is compounded for those who seek to escape the confines of sex-role definitions of their identity. They are subjected to the added pressure to regress and conform, a phenomenon marked by the various forms of social harassment endemic in the 1990s. For these reasons, recovery programs need to include consciousness-raising experiences and the support of consciousness-raised groups. Liberation from the coercive power of a culture addicted to control is as essential as liberation from the power of substance addiction.

In a culture ruled by sex-role stereotyping, the aged have no place; they are no longer capable of exercising masculine competitive power or feminine caregiving; they are no longer considered sexually attractive. The elderly need group support in order to challenge ageism and to rediscover and affirm their worth and value in a milieu which discounts them.

Spiritual Guidance

As stated in Chapter 3, addiction and substance abuse arise ultimately from an attempt to assuage the tension and pain which inheres in being human. However, it has a more proximate source in the suffering that arises from humankind's efforts to control, escape, or deny the limits of finitude. This secondary cause takes the form of oppressive and destructive relational behaviors. The Serenity Prayer, "God, grant me the serenity to accept the things I cannot change, the courage to change the things I can, and the wisdom to know the difference," addresses these two levels of human pain. It differentiates between proximate ills that can be changed and ultimate conditions that must be accepted. It posits the existence of a Power which enables persons to discern the difference between these two realities and to respond appropriately to each. Spirituality can be understood as the search for, the recognition of, and the continuing relationship to that Power. That ultimate reality is named variously as Higher Power, The Sacred, The

Holy, The Source of All Being, God, The Eternal One, Yahweh, The Trinity, Mother God, The Christ, and so forth. The spiritual journey is not undertaken alone but is made in relationship with human forebearers who have made a similar journey and have left us a heritage of the wisdom they have attained, and in relationship with contemporary pilgrims. Recoverers can benefit from the help of spiritual guides who have special gifts and training in the art of spiritual direction. They can, if they are willing to avail of them, find courage, strength, and hope in twelve-step programs such as Pills Anonymous.

Some persons in recovery have been hurt by the inauthentic and oppressive aspects of religions of which they have been a part. Part of recovery involves coming to terms with religions as they have been experienced. Some may still remain members of churches, synagogues, and other religious institutions, others may choose to pursue the spiritual quest without formal membership in any organized religion. Those who remain or return to membership will need to find a way to live their membership with integrity, maintaining an awareness of their ultimate freedom and responsibility before God. They will need the support of others, especially when it is necessary to take a stand against aspects of their religion that are oppressive and that legitimize rather than confront unjust and oppressive secular systems. Women, in particular, need to find support in their search for God images and a religious language which affirms their human worth and dignity.

Persons recovering from medication addiction encounter issues related specifically to concerns of ultimate meaning. They must deal with grief and loss, with matters of guilt, responsibility, hope, forgiveness, and, inevitably, the ultimate meaning of their lives. They should be able to bring these concerns to the pastoral person and expect understanding and help. A spiritual issue of great importance in recovery is the meaning of suffering. Many people, especially women, have been schooled in the erroneous belief that suffering is good in itself and that bearing it unquestioningly is virtuous. Others have fallen prey to the hedonistic doctrine that all pain is to be avoided at all cost. Recovery involves attaining a balanced view of suffering; discerning what can and should be avoided or remedied and what must be accepted. In particular it involves uncovering the experiential meaning of the suffering that cannot be avoided. Various authentic religious traditions (such as the meaning of the Cross in Christianity) supply understandings of such suffering, which can guide recoverers in this search for ultimate meaning.

Recovery for individuals and their families involves an ongoing conversion—not merely cosmetic changes in their lifestyle but a fundamental turn around in attitudes, perceptions, and behavior. This is where continuing pastoral guidance and the support of a faith community is needed. The holistic program of recovery envisioned here is, admittedly, ideal. Restrictions in resources and in finances will make its availability to all who need it difficult to attain. However, it is an ideal worth striving for and is, at least in part, attainable. In this schema, the pastoral caregiver has an important role. Pastoral care specialists, pastoral counselors, pastors, and other ministers are in a pivotal position to initiate and monitor a program such as this, which draws on resources within and outside churches and synagogues. As spiritual guides and pastoral counselors, they are specialists in some of the important dimensions of this comprehensive program such as initial intervention, referral, spiritual guidance, and in giving pastoral support, especially when individuals and families experience difficulties and crises in the course of recovery.

Chapter 6

Prevention

The parable of the fish in the polluted river recounted in the last chapter indicated that a twofold response was necessary in order to save the fish. First, they had to be removed from the river and restored to health; then the river had to be purified of contaminants. The description of a holistic recovery program is the equivalent of the first step in the response. However, the phenomenon of addiction, as Anne Wilson Schaef points out, is not just an individual one; it is a systemic disorder. Prevention of addiction must begin with a recognition of the "addictive" nature of social institutions.

SYSTEMIC REFORM

Pastoral persons should not confine their efforts to treating persons who suffer from various forms of addiction and dependency. They must also work to reform those systems in which they are directly involved. Closest to home are religious institutions, churches, and synagogues. Far from being models of non-addictive communities, these betray symptoms of addiction to power, to pleasure, and to possession. The most pervasive form of power addiction is seen in the lack of equality between males and females which permeates many religious systems. Some theologies legitimize this inequality by subscribing to a literal understanding of the masculine images of God, thereby justifying a dominate-subordinate relationship between male and female in religious organizations and in family systems. Sexual abuse and sexual harassment are the more virulent symptoms of the abuse of power. However, the refusal to give equal voice to men and women, lay and clerical, within religious organizations is a more subtle form of power abuse because it is more easily legitimized theologically, once one accepts the theological premise that maleness is fundamental to the divinity.

Addiction to pleasure would seem at first glance to be quite incompatible with religious institutions. Most preach against pleasure while extolling the virtue of self-denial. However, where there is a faulty theology of suffering that makes it a good in itself, and a rigidly negative attitude toward licit pleasure, there is likely to be a hidden addiction to pleasure. What is denounced publicly (such as sexual promiscuity or gluttony) is practiced privately, sometimes by those most loud in its denunciation. Pleasure is good when it enriches and enhances life. The enjoyment of such legitimate pleasure and providing it for others is a valid pursuit of religious institutions.

The mutual codependence of affluence and poverty in contemporary society has long been recognized. However, theologies that proclaim liberation, including liberation from subhuman conditions of life, have yet to find central positions within the major religious denominations. At best they are tolerated stepchildren, at worst they are illegitimate outcasts. Whereas God may be said to be on the side of the poor, religious systems are still liable to be the cohorts and the beneficiaries of the affluent. Although some religious systems do take a stand against unjust structures, others are satisfied with practicing charity toward the poor while ignoring the systemic causes of poverty and oppression.

First in the order of business for religious systems is setting to right their own households. Churches and synagogues, as well as individual pastoral caregivers, are wounded healers. They are called to minister to the broken even as they tend to their own wounds. This sense of sinfulness, rather than being a deterrent to ministry, can be a center of compassion and humility from which to reach out to a broken world. Religious institutions in recovery themselves can, with love rather than arrogance, confront secular institutions about their values and practices.

Further, the medical system needs to be called to account regarding irresponsible or unnecessary prescribing of psychotropic drugs, especially when these are offered to women and minorities who should instead be encouraged to take action against oppressive situations rather than to endure them. The health care and medical insurance systems as well as local and federal government need to be confronted regarding the mistreatment of the elderly and the failure of these systems to provide adequately for the poor and for those suffering from chronic mental disorders. In my experience, persons undergoing therapy (especially sexual abuse and incest victims) while being denied hospitalization because they do not have adequate insurance, frequently abuse prescribed drugs in their effort to cope with the pain that attends their therapy. I suspect that many persons admitted to emergency rooms for drug overdose are hidden abuse victims or those receiving inadequate therapy. Persons for whom it is too late to prevent such abuse should be provided with the therapy and the support which will enable them to recover without incurring the added problem of medication dependency.

Pastors and pastoral caregivers should be leaders in their churches and synagogues in advocating values which affect the young and the aging. Elders deserve the wherewithall to live their declining years in dignity either in their homes or in well-run, affordable nursing homes which provide for their physical, psychological, social, and spiritual needs. Pastoral leaders should also nurture cooperative rather than competitive values so that the young will realize that it is not always necessary to win in order to have worth. As noted earlier, false standards of human excellence often underlie the abuse of diet pills and steroids.

Finally, churches and synagogues should be leaders in opposing the oppression and abuse of the weak (children, women, elders, minorities, and the poor) while advocating empowerment, especially empowerment of women. Kerry Treasure and Helen Liao in "Survival Training for Drug Dependent Women" say:

> For many women seeking treatment, drug dependency is simply the most obvious and painful manifestation of the larger female condition: socially encouraged dependency.[1]

The feminist movement has had some success—enough to create a backlash in traditional institutions, among them religious institutions. In some ways the feminist movement has had distinct losses, however. It has failed to improve, to any great extent, the lot of poor women and women of color. In fact, because of the backlash that has accompanied the feminist movement in the last few years, the situation of women has declined in many cases. This is particularly true of women who have retained membership in and continued to be loyal supporters of traditional churches and synagogues. There has been a growing tendency to promote so-called family values, some of which canonize the traditional role of women as self-effacing nurturers. The power of religious institutions to ostracize and even punish women who aspire to be autonomous, to question the hitherto unquestioned, has cowed some if not many women into a compliant silence. Women still suffer in abusive marital relations; they are still raped by the thousands in peacetime and in war; they are still paid less than men for the same work; they are still condemned to two full-time jobs: one outside and one inside the home. Churches not actively opposed to their efforts to improve their lives have settled for a complacent neutrality.

If women are to avoid drug dependency, they need to become liberated from dependency on male-dominated institutions to tell them what to think and how to act. They need to be supported in their efforts to improve their life conditions, to protect themselves from abuse and oppression, and to explore and develop a spirituality that is liberating and self-affirming. What many women ask of their churches is not patronizing protection but space to discover and be who they are, support in their struggle for justice, and above all, a *place* rather than a *role*.

RELIGIOUS RESOURCES

In spite of their flaws, religious systems have the potential to provide structures of belief and practices that enable persons to live the inescapable tensions inherent in the human situation. They have rituals to assist the grieving, heal and reconcile the sinning, strengthen the sick and the dying. When these rituals are celebrated in the context of a caring faith community, which is willing to translate them into love and support, they often obviate the need to resort to the palliative of licit drugs in order to cope with the normal problems of life and with fundamental existential conditions.

Churches and synagogues are in the position of being involved with people in an ongoing relationship from birth to death. Probably no other institution has such ready access to the lives of its members at crucial points in the life cycle. Whereas other psychotherapists only see people when they are already in trouble, pastoral caregivers see them when they can avail of growth-producing preventative care. Churches and synagogues can foster cooperative social relations, provide marriage preparation aimed at healthy egalitarian relationships between partners, promote and provide training in parenting skills for both parents when both are available, and guide families through transitions in the family life cycle (birth of children, adolescence, emptying of the nest, midyears, retirement, old age, and death). They are also in a position to give support to single parents, both women and men.

Religions also have an untapped wealth of spirituality. Ministers, priests, and rabbis ought to be specialists in spiritual guidance so that persons may be enabled to discover and personalize the spiritual wisdom of their various religious traditions. Of particular importance is the meaning of suffering in human life. Admittedly, the mystery of suffering will never be fully elucidated. Nevertheless, it is possible to discern suffering that leads to a fuller life from suffering that diminishes life. Addiction is an attempt at alleviating suffering, but it is a perceived remedy that leads to a diminishment of life. It seems to me that contemporary Western culture suffers from the illusion that life should and can be pain free. This illusion is entertained even as the dominant culture causes or takes no steps to assuage suffering which could be alleviated. A foundation for a nonaddictive society is a lived understanding of the purifying and life-giving power of the kind of suffering that purges out arrogance and generates compassion. In a healthy religious system, there is no place for unnecessary suffering, especially that which arises from oppressive religious attitudes and mores.

HELPING INDIVIDUALS

In Chapter 1, I delineated groups particularly vulnerable to legal drug abuse: youth, women, elders, and the poor. As well as seeking to foster a salubrious social and religious climate, pastoral caregivers can be alert to situations and occasions in which preventative action might be taken. The vignettes at the beginning of the first chapter describe the lapse into addiction of a woman who was first prescribed tranquilizers on the tragic death of her husband, a young girl who abused diet pills, a young man who died as a result of abusing steroids, an overmedicated elder in a nursing home. In each of these cases, the early involvement of a knowledgeable pastoral caregiver might have prevented the tragedy of wasted years, of premature death, and of the last years of life spent in a stuporous condition.

Ongoing support including, when necessary, pastoral counseling during times of grief and loss might prevent women such as

Delma from relying on drugs to help them through a sad but normal part of life—losing a loved one in death. Youth groups which build self-esteem and foster wholesome values regarding body image and competition might save some young people like Guadalupe and the young athlete, Greg Johnson, from abusing diet pills and steroids. Support and counsel for families when they have to choose a nursing home for the care of a parent might make it possible for people like Marcia to choose facilities that do not depend on drugs to manage their residents. Pastoral care-givers might help residents of nursing homes to grieve the losses that occur when an elder has to move to a care facility. Pastoral ministry with elders in grief might make it less necessary for personnel to sedate them when they are going through a difficult transition.

As wounded healers, religious institutions are called to seek to forestall harm to their members and heal the wounded even as they attend to their own wounds. Liberating religious institutions are aware of themselves as both holy and flawed, and this aware-ness makes possible an environment in which persons can admit failure without loss of self-esteem and can receive acceptance and encouragement as well as challenge. In liberating religious institutions, the recovery of the individual and the recovery of the system are in constant dialogue and that dialogue gives birth to life.

Notes

Chapter 1

1. "Prescription Drug Abuse and Misuse," *The Michigan Substance Abuse and Traffic Safety Information Center Bulletin* (August 1988).

2. Ibid.

3. "Responsible Prescribing of Controlled Medicines," *American Family Physician 44* (5) (November 1991): 1673-1676.

4. Silverman, Milton, and Philip R. Lee, *Pills, Profits, and Politics.* Los Angeles, CA: University of California Press, 1974: 229.

5. Lambert, Elizabeth, *National Symposium on Medicine and Public Policy.* National Institute on Drug Abuse Notes (Spring/Summer, 1989) 44.

6. "Steroids Widely Abused by Young Athletes," *Chemical People Newsletter* (May/June 1991): 6.

7. Willis, Judith L., "How to Take Weight Off (and Keep It Off) Without Getting Ripped Off," *FDA Consumer,* no. FDA 90-1116 (July-August 1985; updated reprint 1990).

8. "Steroids Widely Abused": 6.

9. Hecht, Annabel, "Tranquilizers: Use, Abuse, Dependency," *FDA Consumer* 70, no. 3084 (October 1978, reprint 1979).

10. Winger, Gail, "Valium, the Tranquil Trap," in *The Encyclopedia of Psychoactive Drugs*, Solomon H. Snyder, MD, ed. New York: Chelsea House Publishers, 1986: 77.

11. Hecht, Annabel, "Tranquilizers: Use, Abuse, Dependency."

12. Harlow, Kirk C., "Patterns of Prescription Drug Mortality in Texas: 1976-1986," *Journal of Drug Issues 21*, (3) (Summer 1991): 543.

13. Silverman, Harold M., eds. *The Pill Book.* New York: Bantam Books, 1994: 993.

14. Cited in "Benzodiazepine Prescribing Down," *American Medical News* (November 11, 1991).

15. Resch, Joseph, and Jane M. Christiansen, *Older Adult Substance Abuse.* Lansing, MI: Michigan Office of Substance Abuse, 1983: 1,2.

16. Cited in Snyder, Karyn, "Seniors and Switches," *Drug Topics* (December 9, 1996): 74.

17. Ibid.

18. Cited in Koski, Keigo, Heikke Luukinen, Pekka Laippala, and Sirkka-Liisa Kivela, "Physiological Factors and Medications as Predictors of Injurious Falls by Elderly People: A Prospective Population-Based Study," *Age and Aging* 29 (January 1996): 29.

19. Ibid.: 29-38.

20. Trinkoff, Alison M., James C. Anthony, and Alvaro Muñoz, "Predictors of Initiation of Psychotherapeutic Medicine Use," *The American Journal of Public Health 80*,(1) (January 1990): 61.

21. Darboe, Momodou N., Gerald Keenan, and Tamara Richards, "The Abuse of Dextromethorphan-Based Cough Syrup: A Pilot Study of the Community of Waynesboro, Pennsylvania," *Adolescence 31* (123) (Fall 1996): 633-644.

Chapter 2

1. Green, Helen l. and Michael H. Levy, *Drug Misuse . . . Human Abuse.* New York: Mercel, Decker, 1976: 449,450.

2. Ibid.: 331,332.

3. Calhoun, Sarah R., "Abuse of Flunitrazepam (Rohypnol) and Other Benzodiazepines in Austin and South Texas," *Journal of Psychoactive Drugs 28* (2) (April-June 1996): 183-189.

4. For a strong critique of antidepressants see Breggin, Peter, MD, *Toxic Psychiatry.* New York: St. Martin Press, 1991.

5. Green and Levy, *Drug Misuse:* 280.

6. Brenton, Myron, *Women and Abuse of Prescription Drugs.* New York: Public Affairs Press, 1982: 12.

7. Willis, Judith Levine, "How to Take Weight Off (and Keep It Off) Without Being Ripped Off," *FDA Consumer* 90, no. 1116 (July/August 1985, updated and reprinted 1990).

8. Rogers, Katie, "Girth Control," *Drug Topics* (May 20, 1996): 30.

9. Cited in Miller, Roger W., "Athletes and Steroids, Playing a Deadly Game," *FDA Consumer* 88, no. 3170 (November 1987).

10. "Steroids Widely Abused by Young Athletes," *Chemical People Newsletter* (May/June 1991).

11. Silverman, Milton and Philip Lee, *Pills, Profits, and Politics.* Los Angeles, CA: University of California Press, 1974: 227.

12. "Quackery Targets Teens," *FDA Consumer Magazine* (Reprinted from February 1988; Revised April 1990).

13. Darboe, Momodou N., Gerald Keenan, and Tamara Richards, "The Abuse of Dextromethorphan-Based Cough Syrup: A Pilot Study of the Community of Waynesboro, Pennsylvania," *Adolescence 31* (123) (Fall 1996): 632-638.

14. Cited by Katie Rogers in *Drug Topics* (August 19, 1996).

15. "Quackery Targets Teens," 4.

16. Fox, Vernelle, MD, "Substance Abuse: Mechanics and Management," (Paper presented to the World Congress of International Rehabilitation Medicine, Mexico City, October 1974): 1.

17. Brenton, *Women and Abuse of Prescription Drugs:* 93.

18. Ibid.: 100.

19. Clinebell, Howard J., *Understanding and Counseling the Alcoholic.* Nashville, TN: Abingdon, 1968: 43-60.

Chapter 3

1. Clinebell, Howard J., *Understanding and Counseling the Alcoholic.* Nashville, TN: Abingdon, 1968: 60.

2. Schaef uses the terms "addict" and "addiction" in a broader sense than this author. She considers all radical dependency on a substance or on a process to be addiction and those under the power of that dependency to be addicts.

3. Schaef, Anne Wilson, *When Society Becomes an Addict.* San Francisco: Harper and Row, 1987: 7-18.

4. Ibid.: 18.

5. Reed, Beth Glover, "Intervention Strategies for Drug Dependent Women," *Treatment Services for Drug Dependent Women,* George W. Beschner et al., eds. Rockville, MD: National Institute on Drug Abuse, 1980: 7.

6. Ibid.: 8.

7. Cited in Reed, "Intervention Strategies": 8,9.

8. August, Paula Nordstrom, "Drugs and Women," in *The Encyclopedia of Psychoactive Drugs*, Solomon H. Snyder, MD, ed. New York: Chelsea House, 1986: 26.

9. Ibid.: 30.

10. Cooperstock, Ruth, "Women and Psychotrophic Drugs," in *Women, Their Use of Alcohol and Other Legal Drugs,* Anne MacLennan, ed. Toronto: Addiction Research Foundation of Toronto, 1976: 83.

11. Brenton, Myron *Women and Abuse of Prescription Drugs.* New York: Public Affairs Press, 1982: 2,3.

12. Cooperstock, *Women, Their Use of Alcohol*: 91.

13. Ibid.: 87.

14. Ibid.: 88.

15. Schaef, *When Society Becomes an Addict*, 50.

16. Lennard, Henry, *Mystification and Drug Abuse.* San Francisco: Jossey-Bass, 1971.

17. Silverman, Milton and Philip Lee, *Pills, Profits, and Politics.* Los Angeles, CA: University of California Press, 1974: 224.

18. For an extended discussion of the hazards of OTCs see Silverman and Lee, 203-233.

19. Orbach, Susan, *Fat Is a Feminist Issue.* New York: Paddington Press, 1978: 28.

20. See Erikson, Erik, *The Life Cycle Completed* (1982); also *Identity: Youth and Crisis* (1968); and *Insight and Responsibility* (1964). New York: W.W. Norton.

21. Cited in Christensen, Jane, "Older Adults," in *Effective Substance Abuse Counseling with Specific Population Groups*, Virginia S. Ryan, PhD, ed. Michigan Department of Public Health, Center for Substance Abuse Services, reprinted September 1993: 11-1.

22. Resch, Joseph E. and Jane M. Christensen, *Older Adult Substance Abuse.* Lansing, MI: Michigan Office of Substance Abuse Services, 1983: 19.

23. Erikson, Erik, *The Life Cycle Completed:* 61-66.

24. Beavers, Robert, "Healthy, Midrange and Severely Dysfunctional Families," in *Normal Family Processes,* Froma Walsh, ed. New York: Guilford Press, 1982: 45-66.

25. Ibid.: 61,62.

26. Cuskey, Walter R. and Richard B. Wathey, *Female Addictions.* Lexington, MA: Health, 1982: 135-137.

27. See Ibid.: 137.

28. Bepko, Claudia, "Disorders of Power: Women and Addiction in the Family," in *Women in Families: A Framework for Family Therapy*, Monica McGoldrick, Carol M. Anderson, and Froma Walsh, eds. New York: W.W. Norton and Company: 420.

Chapter 4

1. Rahner, Karl, *Nature and Grace.* New York: Sheed and Ward, 1963: 138.

2. Schaef, Anne Wilson, *When Society Becomes an Addict.* San Francisco: Harper and Row, 1987: 7.

3. Ibid.: 8.

4. Christ, Carol, *Diving Deep and Surfacing: Women Writers on Spiritual Quest.* Boston: Beacon Press, 1980: 214.

5. Ibid.: 29.

6. Ibid.: 215.

7. Goldstein, Valerie Saiving, "The Human Situation: A Feminist Viewpoint," in *The Nature of Man*, Simon Doniger, ed. Plainview, NY: Books for Libraries Press, 1973: 163.

8. Ibid.

Chapter 5

1. Ryan, Virginia S., *Effective Substance Abuse Counseling with Specific Groups.* Lansing, MI: Michigan Office of Substance Abuse, 1993: 19.

2. Miller, Roger W., "Athletes and Steroids: Playing a Deadly Game," *FDA Consumer* no. 88-3170 (November 1987): 3.

3. Bepko, Claudia, "Disorders of Power: Women and Addiction in the Family," in *Women in Families: A Framework for Family Therapy*, Monica McGoldrick et al., eds. New York: W.W. Norton, 1991: 419.

4. Ibid.: 420

Chapter 6

1. Treasure, Kerry and Helen Liso, "Survival Skills Training for Drug Dependent Women," in *Treatment Services for Drug Dependent Women*, Beth Glover, George M. Beschner, and Josette Mondonaro, eds. Washington, DC: U.S. Department of Health and Human Services, eds. (1982).

Bibliography

August, Paula Nordstrom, "Drugs and Women." In *The Encyclopedia of Psychoactive Drugs,* Solomon H. Snyder, MD, ed. New York: Chelsea House, 1986.

Beavers, W. Robert, "Healthy, Midrange and Severely Dysfunctional Families." In *Normal Family Processes*, Froma Walsh, ed. New York: Guilford Press, 1982.

"Benzodiazepine Prescribing Down," *American Medical News.* November 11, 1991.

Bepko, Claudia, "Disorders of Power: Women and Addiction in the Family." In *Women in Families: A Framework for Family Therapy*, Monica McGoldrick, Carol M. Anderson, and Froma Walsh, eds. New York: W. W. Norton, 1991.

Beschner, George, Reed, Beth Glover, and Josette Mondonaro, eds. *Treatment Services for Drug Dependent Women*, Vols. I and II. United States Department of Health and Human Services, 1981.

Booth, Leo, *When God Becomes a Drug.* New York: Putnam, 1991.

Brenton, Myron, *Women and Abuse of Prescribed Drugs.* New York: Public Affairs Press, 1982.

Christ, Carol, *Diving Deep and Surfacing: Women Writers on Spiritual Quest.* Boston: Beacon Press, 1980.

Clinebell, Howard J., *Understanding and Counseling the Alcoholic.* Nashville, TN: Abingdon, 1968.

Cooperstock, Ruth, "Women and Psychotropic Drugs." In *Women, Their Use of Alcohol and Other Legal Drugs*, Anne MacLennan, ed. Toronto: Addiction Research Foundation of Toronto, 1978.

Cuskey, Walter R. and Richard B. Wathey, "A Model of Female Addiction." In *Female Addictions.* Lexington, MA: Health, 1982.

Erikson, Erik, *Identity, Youth and Crisis.* New York: W. W. Norton, 1968.

_____, *Insight and Responsibility.* New York: W. W. Norton, 1964.

_____, *The Life Cycle Completed.* New York: W. W. Norton, 1982.

Friedman, R.J. and M.M. Katz, eds., "Depression and Learned Helplessness." In *The Psychology of Depression.* Washington, DC: Winston Press, 1974.

Ford, Betty, *The Time of My Life.* New York: Ballantine Books, 1978.

Goldstein, Valerie Saiving, "The Human Situation: A Feminist Viewpoint." In *The Nature of Man*, Simon Doniger, ed. Plainview, NY: Books for Libraries Press, 1973.

Gordon, Barbara, *I'm Dancing as Fast as I Can.* New York: HarperCollins, 1979.

Green, Helen I. and Michael Levy, *Drug Misuse . . . Human Abuse.* New York: Mercel, Decker, 1976.

Hecht, Annabel, "Tranquilizers: Use, Abuse, Dependency," *FDA Consumer* 79-3084, reprint, October 1978 .

Hughes, Richard and Robert Brewin, *The Tranquilizing of America*. New York: Harcourt, Brace, Jovanovich, 1979.

Lambert, Elizabeth, *National Institute on Drug Abuse Notes* (Spring/Summer, 1989).

Lennard, Henry, *Mystification and Drug Abuse*. San Francisco: Jossey-Bass, 1971.

McGoldrick, Monica, et al., eds., *Women in Families: A Framework for Family Therapy*. New York: W.W. Norton, 1991.

Miller, Roger W., "Athletes and Steroids: Playing a Deadly Game," *FDA Consumer* 88-3170 (November 1987).

Nellis, Muriel, *The Female Fix*. New York: Penguin Books, 1980.

Orbach, Susan, *Fat Is a Feminist Issue*. New York: Paddington Press, 1978.

Rahner, Karl, *Nature and Grace*. New York: Sheed and Ward, 1963.

Reed, Beth Glover, "Intervention Strategies for Drug Dependent Women." In *Treatment Services for Drug Dependent Women Vols. I and II*. George Beschner, Beth Glover Reed, and Josette Mondonaro, eds. Rockville, MD: National Institute on Drug Abuse, 1980.

Resch, Joseph E., Jr. and Jane M. Christensen, *Older Adult Substance Abuse*. Lansing, MI: Michigan Office of Substance Abuse Services, 1982.

"Responsible Prescribing of Controlled Medicines," *American Family Physician* 44 (5) (November 1991).

Ryan, Virginia S., *Effective Substance Abuse Counseling with Specific Groups*. Lansing, MI: Michigan Office of Substance Abuse Services, 1993.

Silverman, Milton and Philip Lee, *Pills, Profits, and Politics*. Los Angeles, University of California Press, 1976.

"Steroids Widely Abused by Young Athletes," *Chemical People Newsletter* (May/June, 1991).

The Michigan Substance Abuse and Information Center, "Prescription Drugs, Abuse and Misuse." Lansing, MI: The Michigan Substance Abuse and Traffic Safety Information Center, 1988.

Treasure, Kerry and Helen Liso, "Survival Skills Training for Drug Dependent Women." In *Treatment Services for Drug Dependent Women*. Beth Glover Reed, et al., eds. 1980.

Voth, Eric A., Dupont, Robert L., and Voth, Harold M, eds. "Responsible Prescribing of Controlled Medicines," *American Family Physician* 44, (5) (November 1991).

Willis, Judith, "How to Take Weight Off and Keep It Off without Being Ripped Off," *FDA Consumer* 90, (1116) (July/August, 1985).

Winger, Gail, "Valium: The Tranquil Trap." In *Encyclopedia of Psychoactive Drugs*, Solomon H. Snyder, MD, ed. New York: Chelsea House, 1986.

Index

Order Your Own Copy of
This Important Book for Your Personal Library!

HIDDEN ADDICTIONS
A Pastoral Response to the Abuse of Legal Drugs

_____ in hardbound at $29.95 (ISBN: 0-7890-0266-3)

_____ in softbound at $19.95 (ISBN: 0-7890-0267-1)

COST OF BOOKS_____

OUTSIDE USA/CANADA/
MEXICO: ADD 20%_____

POSTAGE & HANDLING_____
*(US: $3.00 for first book & $1.25
for each additional book)
Outside US: $4.75 for first book
& $1.75 for each additional book)*

SUBTOTAL_____

IN CANADA: ADD 7% GST_____

STATE TAX_____
*(NY, OH & MN residents, please
add appropriate local sales tax)*

FINAL TOTAL_____
*(If paying in Canadian funds,
convert using the current
exchange rate. UNESCO
coupons welcome.)*

☐ **BILL ME LATER:** ($5 service charge will be added)
(Bill-me option is good on US/Canada/Mexico orders only;
not good to jobbers, wholesalers, or subscription agencies.)

☐ Check here if billing address is different from
shipping address and attach purchase order and
billing address information.

Signature_____

☐ **PAYMENT ENCLOSED: $**_____

☐ **PLEASE CHARGE TO MY CREDIT CARD.**

☐ Visa   ☐ MasterCard   ☐ AmEx   ☐ Discover
☐ Diner's Club

Account # _____

Exp. Date _____

Signature _____

Prices in US dollars and subject to change without notice.

NAME _____

INSTITUTION _____

ADDRESS _____

CITY _____

STATE/ZIP _____

COUNTRY _____ COUNTY (NY residents only) _____

TEL _____ FAX _____

E-MAIL_____
May we use your e-mail address for confirmations and other types of information? ☐ Yes   ☐ No

Order From Your Local Bookstore or Directly From
The Haworth Press, Inc.
10 Alice Street, Binghamton, New York 13904-1580 • USA
TELEPHONE: 1-800-HAWORTH (1-800-429-6784) / Outside US/Canada: (607) 722-5857
FAX: 1-800-895-0582 / Outside US/Canada: (607) 772-6362
E-mail: getinfo@haworth.com
PLEASE PHOTOCOPY THIS FORM FOR YOUR PERSONAL USE.

BOF96

FORTHCOMING and NEW BOOKS
IN RELIGION, MINISTRY & PASTORAL CARE

WHAT THE DYING TEACH US

Lessons on Living
Reverend Samuel Lee Oliver, BCC
A collection of actual experiences and insights shared by terminally ill persons.
$29.95 hard. ISBN: 0-7890-0475-5.
$14.95 soft. ISBN: 0-7890-0476-3.
Available Summer 1998. Approx. 114 pp. with Index.
Features personal reflections on death and dying.

SPIRITUAL CRISIS

Surviving Trauma to the Soul
J. LeBron McBride, PhD
Discover how you can reverse the impact of spiritual crisis and apply healing balm to the traumatized soul.
$39.95 hard. ISBN: 0-7890-0135-7.
$19.95 soft. ISBN: 0-7890-0460-7.
Available Spring 1998. Approx. 282 pp. with Index.
Features case studies, tables, and figures.

HIDDEN ADDICTIONS

A Pastoral Response to the Abuse of Legal Drugs
Bridget Clare McKeever, PhD, SSL
Shows you the social roots of addiction and gives you the spiritual and religious resources necessary to put you and your loved ones on the road to holistic recovery.
$29.95 hard. ISBN: 0-7890-0266-3.
$14.95 soft. ISBN: 0-7890-0267-1.
Available Spring 1998. Approx. 149 pp. with Index.
Features case studies and a bibliography.

UNDERSTANDING CLERGY MISCONDUCT IN RELIGIOUS SYSTEMS

Scapegoating, Family Secrets, and the Abuse of Power
Candace R. Benyei, PhD
Helps you see leaders of religious institutions in a way that the world has been afraid to see them—in a glass clearly.
$29.95 hard. ISBN: 0-7890-0451-8.
$19.95 soft. ISBN: 0-7890-0452-6.
Available Spring 1998. Approx. 203 pp. with Index.
Features a glossary and appendixes.

THE EIGHT MASKS OF MEN

A Practical Guide in Spiritual Growth for Men of the Christian Faith
Rev. Dr. Frederick G. Grosse
This book will encourage you to come out from behind your mask of solitude and loneliness—one of man's most obtrusive masks—and reach out for help and community.
$39.95 hard. ISBN: 0-7890-0415-1.
$19.95 soft. ISBN: 0-7890-0416-X.
Available Winter 1997/98. Approx. 181 pp. with Index.
Features anecdotal stories and excerpts by men who have undergone spiritual group work and an appendix of biblical references for spiritual growth.

WHEN LIFE MEETS DEATH

Stories of Death and Dying, Truth and Courage
Thomas William Shane, DDiv
A book of stories from people who have faced the ordinary, yet overwhelming, experience of the death of a loved one.
$24.95 hard. ISBN: 0-7890-0289-2.
1997. Available now. 146 pp. with Index.

THE HEART OF PASTORAL COUNSELING

Healing Through Relationship, Revised Edition
Richard Dayringer, ThD
On the first edition:
"A comprehensive volume that offers concrete help and provides ladders for those suffering counseling pitfalls."
—*Ministry*
$39.95 hard. ISBN: 0-7890-0172-1
$19.95 soft. ISBN: 0-7890-0421-6.
Available Winter 1997/98. Approx. 209 pp. with Index.
Features 4 appendixes, charts/figures, diagnostic criteria, and a bibliography.

DYING, GRIEVING, FAITH, AND FAMILY

A Pastoral Care Approach
George W. Bowman, III, ThM, BD
Provocative, suggestive, and stimulating to professionals and educators working with and teaching about dying and grieving persons.
$39.95 hard. ISBN: 0-7890-0262-0.
$19.95 soft. ISBN: 0-7890-0263-9.
1997. Available now. 150 pp. with Index.

THE PASTORAL CARE OF DEPRESSION

A Guidebook
Binford W. Gilbert, PhD
Shows pastors how to help people who come to them in a state of depression.
$29.95 hard. ISBN: 0-7890-0264-7.
$14.95 soft. ISBN: 0-7890-0265-5.
1997. Available now. 127 pp. with Index.

A GOSPEL FOR THE MATURE YEARS

Finding Fulfillment by Knowing and Using Your Gifts
Harold G. Koenig, MD, Tracy Lamar, MDiv, and Betty Lamar, BFA

Guides middle-aged and older adults toward emotional and spiritual growth, joy, and satisfaction in their mature years regardless of their circumstances, health, or age.
$39.95 hard. ISBN: 0-7890-0158-6.
$19.95 soft. ISBN: 0-7890-0170-5. 1997. Available now. 148 pp.

Faculty: Textbooks are available for classroom adoption consideration on a 60-day examination basis. You will receive an invoice payable within 60 days along with the book. If you decide to adopt the book, your invoice will be cancelled. Please write to us on your institutional letterhead, indicating the textbook you would like to examine as well as the following information: course title, current text, enrollment, and decision date.

The Haworth Pastoral Press
An imprint of the The Haworth Press, Inc.
10 Alice Street
Binghamton, New York 13904–1580 USA

Visit our online catalog and search
for publications of interest to you by
title, author, keyword, or subject!
http://www.haworth.com

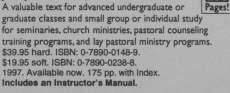